NOTHING
HAPPENS BY
ACCIDENT!

COVER PICTURE

Francesca da Rimini by William Dyce, 1806–64 by kind permission of the National Gallery of Scotland.

The story behind the painting is that Francesca, married to an elderly and deformed husband, falls in love with his younger brother Paolo, while reading to him. In its original format, Dyce's composition included, on the far left, the figure of the husband creeping in to murder the lovers by stealth, but the painting was later trimmed.

What do we have represented here in spiritual terms? Is the falling in love an accident? No, all our personal relationships are intended events. Then why the cruel circumstances, leading to retribution from the aged husband? This is life-plan. The moon and the planet (Venus?) in the sky are suggestive of other influences at work. If Francesca and Paolo were spiritual thirds, they would be drawn to each other like moths to a flame, even if that meant painful consequences. A not uncommon test is to meet and marry, and then later one's true soul-mate appears. The crossroads choice presented is whether to stay faithful or go with the heart.

The composition is very representative of spiritual thirds – bringers of both joy and grief to one's life. One will always meet one's third. Where destined to be partners, thirds will share a telepathy, a knowingness that is different to the relationships of others. This characterises a spiritual third. For the woman, upon meeting for the first time, recognition is often in the eyes.

NOTHING HAPPENS BY ACCIDENT!

SPIRITUAL INSIGHTS INTO
LIFE'S DRAMA

ROGER J BURMAN

Quiet Waters Publishing Ltd

First published in 2003

British Library Cataloguing in Publication Data

A catalogue record for this book is available from the British
Library

ISBN 0-9542047-2-7

Typeset by CityScape Books
www.cityscapebooks.co.uk

Published by Quiet Waters Publishing Ltd
North Lodge, The Pines, Boston Road
Sleaford, Lincolnshire NG34 7DN
Publishing@bssk.co.uk

Printed and bound in Great Britain
By Antony Rowe, Eastbourne

CONTENTS

INTRODUCTION

Perhaps the most arresting realisation one can have is that
consciousness can exist independently of the body. Very few will
arrive at that realisation, but for those that do the change can be
profound in the way they look at life and the world. The
realisation does not provide answers, but it is the equivalent of
stumbling across the alchemist's elusive formula that might
transform base metal into gold and give rise to the discovery of the
philosopher's stone; it is the key to a new understanding of life. It
allows one to see that we are in fact spirit beings first and
foremost, having a human experience for, what in the scheme of
things, is only a few short years!

We are all spirit. How do I evidence that? It is not my purpose
to do so as there are many others tasked with that. There are
many books available written by mediums and healers, which
document near death experiences, the evidence for reincarnation
and so on. Should one require evidence in addition to books, there
are the complementary therapy centres which are now springing
up in most population centres, where one can experience an
improvement in one's health or mental well-being that the
scientists find difficult to explain. Secondly, there are the
mediums who give readings from spirit or platform
demonstrations of spiritual communication. Thirdly, there is
internal evidence in meditation experiences some people have, of
spirit communication or past life memories. External evidence is
now more common with spirit being captured by digital cameras.
However, I am told by the guides that coming to an awareness of
spirit must be an individual quest or it is not meaningful.

Who is writing this book? I sometimes switch from singular "I"
to plural "we". The "we" will refer to my partner Angela and
myself, or Angela, our guide and myself. It is difficult to separate
the authorship. I have put the book together but the material for
it has come through Angela's mediumship. In a sense therefore
we are joint authors. The spirit communication is from our joint

guide as Angela and I are the two incarnated parts of a spiritual three. A "three" becomes a "one" in the spirit state and only subdivides for the purpose of incarnations. Therefore the book is from one spirit entity, in effect. One of the tasks for spirit when it is ready to undertake it is to be teachers of others and bringers of new information to the place of incarnation, which in our case is Earth, but that is only one of many planets used by spirit. We pre-planned in our spirit state, to write our books as part of this, our task in this incarnation.

Who is the intended reader? The book will hopefully find its way to those who have never had, or no longer have, an unquestioning acceptance of an unanswering God in the Christian image, but who cannot blindly substitute that there is a rational-scientific explanation to life and every phenomenon in it. Science has played its role in freeing the Western mind from the stranglehold of Christianity, but now it is time for science to exit centre stage and for greater knowledge and belief in spirit and the spiritual dimension to return to being the leading actor, as it was before the arrival of religions.

The book may not find all of its intended audience for some time. Today, there are many children of great spirituality alive on the planet. They have come to help the world raise its vibration to the next level, and more are being born all the time. They will question the accepted ways and conventions. They will have more recognition of their true spiritual nature than any before them. They will no doubt face criticism and derision for their beliefs, but hopefully, in the future, this book will serve as confirmation for them that they are correct in their inner knowledge, and that there are others that share their hopes with them. Indeed, some will go further and into more depth in their own writings than I have been allowed to do here.

My purpose and the purpose of this book is to explain why we, as spiritual beings, need to have human experiences. All of us are energy systems. The events of any one life are transitory and of no real and lasting effect to the spirit that is within. However, we are born with our accumulated knowledge temporarily blocked and so this realisation is most difficult to appreciate; indeed, the majority of the population will not do so as it is not the time that they should. Reincarnation is nevertheless a key feature of the spiritual journey.

We need not fear that as our bodies wear out doomsday approaches. We are going to be born into a new body with new parents! Readers of *"Why Come Back? Book Two"* will know that I have described my own fourteen past lives on Earth. This is a relatively low number for earthly incarnations and only a small fraction of my total lives. One of the most significant changes of perspective is to see each other, not as being biologically young or old, but to see ourselves as being young, middle-aged or older spirit. Our spiritual ages are vastly different from our biological ones. Instead of measuring ourselves in units of Earthly years between one and a century, we should see ourselves, in many cases at least, as many thousands of years old and this lifetime but one of hundreds that we will experience along our spiritual journey.

I am told by spirit that now is not the time to elaborate on my extraterrestrial (ET) lives. I am, however, accumulating instances of ET lives which are recalled by participants in my past life regression workshops. I also have a family member who can, by means of spirit communication, paint landscapes of other worlds that spirit uses for incarnation and hope that I may be allowed to use this evidence in a future book. For now, my task is to explain the hidden workings of spirit in our human experience lives.

I would like to quote Cassius' words to Brutus in Shakespeare's *"Julius Caesar"*:

> *"And since you know you cannot see yourself*
> *So well as by reflection, I, your glass,*
> *Will modestly discover to yourself*
> *That of yourself which you yet know not of."*

This I aim to do also. There are no accidents in life. Our choice of parents, career, hobbies, the significant people in our lives, for example, will all be planned by us or arranged by our spirit guides. In chapter one, I give further information than is contained in my previous two books concerning the concept of spiritual threes. Chapter two explains more about life-plans which we all have, as without a life-plan there can be no life. In chapter three, I exemplify the unfolding of life-plans using lives of ten famous Britons as illustration. The invisible hand of spirit also manifests itself through the influence of our past lives on the present one. Some of the sometimes surprising and unexpected ways this can occur I discuss in chapter four. We are not alone in this, as animals can have past life influences too, which I illustrate in chapter six.

Chapter five explains why we attract to ourselves the disease that we need by discussing illness from the spiritual perspective. I also give some glimpses into the future. On other more advanced worlds there is no illness, only preventative treatment. As I have written previously, Earth is a "nursery" world that spirit uses, but once the population raises its vibration sufficiently, the planet will move on and the nursery status, of which illness is a feature, will be left behind.

I wish to thank my partner Angela, without whose long hours of mediumship this book would not have been possible. I also wish to thank our enquirers and course attendees who have been the means of me acquiring information beyond my own questioning of spirit, particularly those I have used on an anonymous basis in writing chapter four.

It is my great privilege to present my research and the wisdom I have received from the spirit dimension to you.

April 2003

Quiet Waters
Hull Marina
East Yorkshire
England

CHAPTER ONE

THREE IS THE MAGIC NUMBER

The concept of the Spiritual Three adds an important level of explanation to everyone's time on planet Earth. There is no one who will not be affected by interaction with their third at some point in their life. If the influence is not life-long, it will certainly be life-changing. I introduced the concept in my first book, but perhaps did not expand it sufficiently to show how much it explains the hidden hand of spirit that choreographs our lives. New spiritual information is introduced in pieces to us, and it appears that I have been given the immense privilege of being able to introduce this piece and to write about the Spiritual Three.

I am aware of other writers of spiritual topics who clearly are making reference to a three, or description of it at work, but have not got a clear picture of this building block of spiritual knowledge. One reader of my first book described it as "the missing link", the piece of the jigsaw that once in place enables one to see the whole picture; so much so that what she had previously puzzled over now made a great deal more sense to her.

We all only act a part at this time. This lifetime is only a small segment of the whole being, the equivalent of a second in the scheme of the spiritual journey. All our lives are a series of experiences created to make us a being of pure light, capable of joining the three thirds of ourselves together and moving into the Collective (or other preferred term for God). This is ultimately the ambition of all spirit. I would like to recap the concept of Spirit Threes before proceeding, as a refresher for readers of books one and two, and as necessary basic knowledge for any new readers.

SPIRIT THREES

When an entity splits from The Source (or God, or whatever your preferred term is) to begin its journey, it further sub-divides into three parts. When an incarnation is planned, two of these parts will choose to incarnate while the third stays behind to act as guide for the other two. There is no strict order to this, but all will be guide at some point. There is thus no mystery to spirit guides. We each have been a guide ourselves! The guide is a part of each one of us, although we share the guide with another person whilst both spirits are incarnated.

The two that incarnate will, at some time in their lives, interact. They are spiritual twins, two parts of a whole. The assassinated pop-star, John Lennon, said of his wife Yoko, *"We are two halves"*. He recognised his third, I believe. The interaction may be in many different forms; they may be mother and child, father and child, siblings, life partners, teacher and pupil, nurse and patient, neighbours, childhood and lifelong friends, and so on.

The meeting may be long, such as a mother and child, or it may be brief, as in the case of a nurse and her patient. What is definite, however, is that this meeting will either have a dramatic impact on the lives concerned as in the case of a brief interaction, or be involved in the shaping of the life as in the case of a meeting of longer term.

It may be useful to give Angela's favourite example of a brief meeting here. She is aware of a nurse who had delivered a baby who died within a few minutes of birth. The nurse had seen the mother suffer throughout the whole of her pregnancy, requiring hospitalisation on more than one occasion. She had then had a difficult and extended labour, only to lose the child within moments. The nurse was so affected by this, she left mainstream nursing and followed something she had nurtured within her, but thought never to be more than a vague idea. She moved overseas to nurse with an organisation who works for the relief of children in impoverished areas, what we term "third world" countries.

The baby was the spiritual third of the nurse. The meeting was amazingly brief, but served as the catalyst, as they had pre-planned it would, to set the nurse firmly on the track of her intended destiny. The baby for its part, still being full of its pre-birth spirituality, felt the compassion of the nurse and gained its required experience from this and its time in the womb. (This was the extent of the baby's life-plan. It was not a tragedy in spiritual terms for the life to be so brief).

This is an example of the role of a third. The meeting may be joyous and a deep, moving and loving experience. It may just as likely be cataclysmic as in this example, creating pain or distress, but providing the necessary catalyst to create circumstances that allow each party to fulfil their plan for their lives. That plan will have been written by all parts of the three beforehand. On return to spirit, the first to return will wait with the guide until the last one returns. All three review the lives, learn from them, and if certain areas are unfulfilled, decide how these may be achieved in future lives. After a period together, the next incarnations take place.

This is the spiritual journey. It continues over five spiritual levels and has seven stages within each level. It can take several lifetimes to complete one stage and many lifetimes to complete one level. The whole purpose of the journey is to learn and experience. The goal is to know what in our earthly terms we will refer to as "unconditional love". It is not really an adequate description, but as close as our language allows.

When the journey is complete, the three parts of a spirit entity join together and return to the Collective, God, the Great Spirit, whatever is your preferred term for the One, the "All That Is". (In other places with advanced life, I am told our term God is more commonly known as the Collective). A joined three enriches the Collective with the fruits of its experiences. This can be compared to a bee leaving the hive, collecting nectar on its journey and returning to enrich the community with its offerings.

This hopefully shows the role of the spirit third. Whatever else happens in an incarnation, the one thing that is definite is that you will interact with your other third. The feeling of there being one other soul in the world that is a mate for you, is the inner knowledge of your third. This has given rise to the term "soul mate", which is not incorrect. What is incorrect, however, is the narrow romantic interpretation that has subsequently been given to the term.

Princess Diana, in her famous TV interview revealed her husband's infidelity with the statement, "There were three of us in this marriage, so it was a bit crowded!" Well, for those who have a long term relationship with their incarnated spiritual third, there are indeed three in the relationship. The guide knows every thought of both if he wants to, and certainly every emotion of both.

In the spiritually aware, it is a delight for the guide to spend peaceful moments with his incarnated counterparts.

Knowledge of the spiritual three would have been given to ancient man along with other information about the workings of spirit. This would have possibly been by older spirit having an incarnation here, bringing some of their wisdom, not just of threes, but other knowledge including spiritual healing and communication. Although over time, knowledge of the spiritual dimension, the afterlife and earth energies dwindled, cultures in pre-Roman times, or certainly their priest class, would have had the knowledge of the spiritual three. Thus when Christianity arrived, the concept was adopted and adapted. The concept of the Holy Trinity, of "Father, Son and Holy Ghost", is distorted knowledge of the three. As explained, the roles of the two incarnated parts are not limited to father and child though.

When one understands the significance of the spiritual three, the number three will often arise to point a pathway. We have some friends, met through spiritual connections, who live in a house numbered thirty-three. They have come to realise that when they bought it, their initial feeling that the house was for them, was no false clue. Later on, developing an interest in spiritual matters, we have answered their questions and confirmed that the house is the centre of what was an ancient but powerful energy site. It is to play an important role in their futures. It is not unusual for those who have skill in the healing fields to find themselves living on or near important ancient energy sites. It is often so engineered by spirit, by life-plan, or just because they instinctively feel the magnetism of the place.

Why some marriages are strong and enduring and others weak and brief has been much written about by relationship experts. They are, however, mostly unaware of the spiritual perspective. If you have written it into your life-plans that you will come together with your third and be life partners, then you may well experience a relationship like no other. You will instinctively often share the same thoughts, know what each other is thinking without voicing it, share the same sense of humour and have many common opinions. You will know instinctively if the other is pained or distressed, and equally know when they feel joy. You will encourage and delight in each others personal and spiritual growth.

This is not to say one can only be truly happy in a relationship where both are thirds (unbeknown on a conscious level, but known spiritually). We share lifetimes with other spirits who become familiar to us, especially as we become older spiritually and hence have had more incarnations. If we have a partner with whom we have had long term contact in past lives, this can produce a particularly close link. This point may require a refresher for any new readers, which I now give.

SOUL GROUPS

In addition to your own three, which are separate parts of a whole, you may have certain other spirit entities with which you interact well. These threes may share roles within your life-plan when possible, and so create a familiarity and ease with each other.

If I can use the analogy of a play or film in which the director has the task of casting actors to interact well with his star, then if you view your guide as the director in the play of your life, the task is for him to find other "actors" to work well with his star performers. If he knows of actors from other plays that have worked well and established a rapport with his stars, then, provided they are available at the right time, it makes perfect sense to use them again, rather than choose unknown players who may not work well. This is a huge oversimplification, but for the purpose of illustration, shows the concept.

So it is that groups of souls incarnate into each other's lives on countless occasions. This explains the feeling of "knowing" someone at a deep level when you have in fact only just met them. This can explain the almost telepathic ability of life partners to know how each other will think and react in certain circumstances. They may well have experienced similar situations in the same roles previously. The dramatist changes the props but may keep the same players; so do we as spirits.

Just as partners who antagonise each other may incarnate again and again into the role of partners to assist each other in learning certain lessons, partners who share a deep and loving relationship may also incarnate as partners again and again in order to assist in learning other lessons. The spirit that was a partner in one incarnation may be a parent or child in another. We all experience male and female incarnations throughout our journey, although we are predominantly one gender, so a husband may find himself the wife of the same partner in a future life. These reoccurring lives enable strong bonds and deep loves to be formed between spirits when in earthly incarnation.

One may of course, on occasion, find oneself in a life where you are the only "new boy" in an established cast. This often accounts for the person who feels out of sync with their surroundings and family, but again, this will have been planned for the lessons it teaches. We need to remember that in order to know hot, you also need to understand the nature of cold. Having food does not teach about hunger but the lack of it does. Lessons are often best learned by comparison, and finding yourself surrounded by incompatible people can be for the lessons it can teach.

SOUL MATE

As explained, a soul mate is simply the other part of yourself, a twin of you. (This does not mean that they resemble you or have the same nature or characteristics on the earth plane, although this can sometimes happen; just that they are a twin of your soul on a spiritual level). It does not infer any romantic connection, as this person can be a parent or child, a teacher or pupil. The pre-destined life partner is the one who people are thinking of when they use the term soul mate in an earthly context.

One may have a deep inner knowledge of the other part of oneself out there somewhere waiting for the connection, if that connection is to be in adulthood or in later life. If the connection for a child is a parent, then this feeling may never be experienced, or if one is a "beginner", just starting on the first steps of the spiritual journey, then such inner feelings may not yet have developed. One may just as easily have a deep inner knowledge of a pre-destined romantic partner, and search for this one. Some may know instinctively as soon as they meet, hence the "love at first sight" feelings. Others may grow to this understanding over the weeks and months of acquaintanceship.

This pre-destined partner will be important to a life-plan for both the participants, and the love between them can be deep and meaningful. It can lead to the accruing of much knowledge on the journey to fully know unconditional love. In some circumstances, there may be cataclysmic events attached to these meetings in the same way as with the other third, but if there are, it is most likely that this will be the way it was planned, for the accruing of experience.

We had a mediumship enquirer who had great spiritual awareness. As is the case with many couples, her husband was sceptical of spirit. The male of our species often finds it embarrassing and difficult to embrace metaphysical concepts. Her husband felt some hurt when told of the concept of the spiritual three, when his wife had correctly identified and had it confirmed that her son was her third. He felt left out of their special relationship. Here is the consoling message from spirit, given to the husband who we will call Angus. We will refer to the wife as Jean, the son as Thomas and the joint guide of Jean and Thomas as Henry.

"My information here is to be limited to telling you that the two of you have shared incarnations as husband and wife many times. Each of you has experienced both roles. Through this, you have a deep inner knowledge of each other. You have planned in this incarnation to experience a meaningful love of each other, a depth of understanding and mutual nourishment, which is to be cherished and which is the goal of many but is achieved by comparatively few.

All parts of each three have interacted together many times, so Thomas and Henry, as well as Jean, have shared lives with Angus previously, and Angus' guide and other third have shared lives with Thomas, Henry and Jean, too. The threes are closely connected in this way and the association goes back for many hundreds of your years.

In this life, Thomas is a special child and all agreed that it would be of benefit for him to be nurtured in that loving home. It was planned that this would be provided by Jean and Angus, because of the deep love they could generate having had "practice at it" in previous incarnations. Angus and his other thirds were just as much involved in this planning as Jean, Thomas and Henry. His three is following its agenda, which happily complements and assists, and is complemented and assisted by Jean's three.

I am allowed to say that your spirit thirds are delighted with the way you have both followed your destinies to this point and wish to send their love too. It is their hope that the discovery of the information contained herein, will take your joint relationship to even greater depths of love, understanding, mutual nourishment and support; that the knowledge of your shared past will help enrich your shared future. I hope this is of assistance to you and give it with my love and deepest blessings." – Henry

It is familiarity from partner relationships in previous lives that is the key to a strong bond, which can be with another spirit besides one's third. To explain this message to new readers, it is unusual in two respects. Firstly, because of the clarity of her mediumship skill, Angela, my partner, can "take a letter", rather like dictation, and type exactly what she hears. Secondly, her guide has stepped aside to allow this message from Henry to be transmitted direct to her, in contrast to the normal rule of all mediumship being from guide to guide, that is from the guide of the enquirer, to the medium's guide then to the medium.

Just in case the reader is wondering, "How will I meet my third?" the answer is you do not have to do anything. There is no way that thirds will not meet! The guide's role is to ensure that they do. Sometimes the arrival of this person will be by quite a circuitous route, so much so that the wonder will be that the meeting ever occurred, but of course, it was destined.

An example from my own past lives, was my seeing a slave being beaten, thousands of miles from my home country of that life, England, rescuing him and making him my servant. This was in the eighteenth century when I was a sea captain. Neither of us knew at that meeting that we were thirds. What would have happened if I had done nothing and walked on? Would I have failed my life-plan? Well, in book two I have spoken of "Roger's involuntary urges", a compulsion to do something one sometimes experiences, which is prompted by the guide. I have no memory of the event in that life, but I suspect my guide at the time would have given me such an urge, had I not responded voluntarily to rescue the beaten slave.

Another example is that of how Angela and I (both thirds) met in the current life, a question we are sometimes asked. We both had marriages that ended in divorce five years previously. Angela had been living alone, determined not to let a man get close and hurt her again. I had a relationship for four years following the divorce, but found myself single after the relationship ended and used the columns of a local newspaper to advertise for a girlfriend. Angela would never have dreamed of responding to such an advert, particularly as she did not want a relationship, but following a particularly lonely and miserable Christmas, a work colleague of hers became quite insistent she give it a try, even selecting a particular advert (mine) that looked intriguing she thought.

This is another example of guides at work, this time using collusion with a third party's guide to affect the thinking of their incarnated counterpart. Angela took some persuading, but eventually did respond at the second or third urging by this colleague, thinking the person behind the advert would most likely be unsuitable, but if he were not, she would keep things at a distance, and would look for friendship only. She was still adamant she did not want a relationship, just a friend to share outings and celebrations. At our first meeting, she had an instant "recognition" of me at some deep, inner level. As is often the case for the male, I did not immediately feel the same inner recognition, but did find myself captivated by her obvious spirituality.

The timing of the meeting of thirds is controlled by the guide. Sometimes there are preparation experiences required. In the case of old spirit who have a destiny working spiritually in some way, we have noticed that the thirds have not met until both had achieved a certain progression and journeyed a certain way alone, so that when they did in fact meet, they were at the correct state of acceptance and understanding of their spirituality to go forward from that point.

Finally, a word of caution here is that although the meeting will happen, what happens afterwards is down to freewill choice. We are aware of this from two lady mediumship enquirers whose lives are in an emotional turmoil because they have met their third, but the relationship has ended by the other party's decision. There was not much in the way of practical advice to give, but some comfort offered by the guides was the news the other party in both cases, is not settled and knows at a deeper level, that there is something missing in their lives.

SOME CASE STUDIES CONCERNING THIRDS

I would now like to give some examples from our mediumship
cases of the search for one's third during the lifetime. Many young
lady enquirers present questions of the "fortune-telling" variety,
wanting to know about future husbands, future homes, number of
children and so on. The guides will not always answer these
questions, as it may be inappropriate to give the answers. Rather
like sitting an exam with the answer paper in front of you, you
would undoubtedly know the answers, but where would be the
achievement? Sometimes, however, particularly if the enquirer
has taken steps to try and spot their own pathway or destiny, the
guide will answer, or perhaps give broad hints.

My first case study involved a lady I shall call Lesley, who
asked if she had met her husband to be yet. Her guide replied
that she had. She then said that she had a long-term relationship
with Garry, but a relationship that is intermittent. She was
attracted to David, and is now confused. Here is her guide's
counsel:

*"This is the whole purpose of Lesley finding her way here today,
and Alberik (her guide) is quite pleased that she has. It is the
purpose of her incarnation and the incarnation of her third, to get
this correct in this life. They have a past life situation which keeps
reappearing in subsequent incarnations, and they need to break the
cycle this time.*

*Lesley and Garry are spiritual thirds. This means they have
shared many lives together, in varying roles. In their last three
joint incarnations, and again in this one, they were intended to be
partners. In the first of the three lives, within two days of their
marriage, a disaster occurred which has left a fingerprint on the
subsequent incarnations. In each since that time, as they approach
a stage of commitment, they draw back, their unconscious
fingerprint memory from the past stopping them going forward. It
is hoped in this life, that they can overcome finally this problem,
and so move forward. They are intended to commit to each other
this time.*

*David is one from a past incarnation that Lesley had a liaison
with. She is feeling the remembered attraction from this time. It is
not planned that they have a repeat of this liaison in this*

incarnation. Lesley should not feel any problem about the attraction, but it should be just that, an attraction.

If she and Garry succeed in overcoming this blockage, they will find that their lives are enriched this time as they will be in a position to achieve the part of their plan that requires them to be in a committed relationship to achieve. In a spiritual sense, they will also be able to progress to the next part of their journey on return to spirit.

The word "fingerprint" here, refers to a trace memory. I devote chapter four to a discussion of how our past lives can influence the current one. To continue my case studies, another young lady whom I shall call Janet, had a similar line of enquiry. Janet had met a young man, Robert. Her guide said this was to be a friend, but is not intended to be a partner this time. He does bear similarities to the one who is to be her partner this time, however, which is part of the attraction for her. Her guide went on to say this:

Janet is fortunate that her life-partner for the incarnation is to be her spiritual third. This is a special relationship that cannot be fully understood unless you are privileged to experience it. They will meet as a result of her work and of her being in Scotland. This is some way off yet however, we envisage it being towards the end of next year, although time is always difficult for us.

Janet has chosen, as part of her plan this time, to feel her own strength. To love herself for her strengths, recognise them within herself and hold true to her ideals. When she forms her new relationship, it will be mutually fulfilling, mutually respecting and with a partner of equal strength of character and purpose. They will not require security in the form of marriage, but will find it in the bond they have, which needs no earthly form of security to cement it.

Janet will instinctively know her third when they meet, it will be as if she has known this person forever, which indeed she has. We cannot give her the name, as part of the spiritual growth is the inner recognition of the spiritual twin of herself. In this relationship she will find the delight of "knowing" her partner, truly knowing as one knows oneself.

It was not in Janet's plan to have children this time. She will always have a love of them, having had the role of mother in many other lifetimes, and having a strong instinct for it, but will use this love towards children not necessarily of her own. Again, we think she has the inner understanding of this. She will not feel that she has missed this in her life, however. Her relationship with her intended partner will be sufficiently rewarding for this not to be a sadness to her.

We would say to Janet, that to date, she has things exactly on track. She is in Scotland, she is meant to be. She is single, she is meant to be. She has cleared her space and is ready for events during this coming year that will lead her to her destined meeting. The reason she has no real attachment to her current home is again an instinctive knowledge that it is only an interim residence for her. Comfortable and a reflection of herself, but not permanent."

Often, when we have explained the concept of the spiritual three, an enquirer will ask, "Who is my third?" As can be seen in this guide's message, this is a question unlikely to be answered. What does receive a yes or no answer, is "Have I met my third yet?" and what will receive a more detailed reply is to seek confirmation about a person already met whom one suspects to be one's third. Unless it is time for them to come together, the guides will not allow a medium to confirm to them that they are thirds. This is only revealed, if it is at all, when the time has come for the lives to join together. This is if the incarnated thirds are to be partners. If the thirds are to be mother and child, siblings or even friends, then they may not be told of their spiritual relationship, or if they are, only at a time when the knowledge will not affect decisions needing to be made in order to complete spiritual progression.

It may be planned that the third will be in a life-partner role, but there is a prior relationship to be experienced, then the meeting of thirds may not immediately follow its end as happened in the case of Angela and myself. Sometimes a gap is planned, so the person has time to feel good about themselves and let go of resentment. A period to regain full confidence and settle in pursuing a new goal perhaps. It may be sometimes destined that the third will be working in this new field chosen, and that they come together through this shared interest.

My next illustration contains words of caution. When spirit gives a prediction of a relationship to come "like no other", it might be erroneous to think of a deeply romantic attachment. Also, one must be aware of having one's attention drawn away from an intended event as a kind of spiritual test. It is possible to encounter red herrings in one's life-plan, written in as a test to see if one has that inner knowingness of one's spiritual third, who may not always be in the role of partner, of course. This happened to me in fact. I started an association with a lady much younger than myself, at about the same time that I met Angela. I knew nothing of the concepts of red herrings, life-plans or spiritual threes at the time, but was compelled towards Angela's spirituality and so passed the test I had set for myself.

Here is a cautionary and cryptic message the guides gave to an enquirer, Daphne, who had received spirit communication through Angela on previous occasions:

"We have said that the meeting will be a catalyst to Daphne's spiritual growth and development and that the relationship will be like no other she has experienced; that it will provide a partner in her work as well as in her personal life. By saying that the relationship will be like no other she has experienced, Daphne assumed that we meant moonlight and roses to use her own phrase. When we use this phrase, or similar words, it can mean that, but it can also mean a relationship that is tumultuous and stirs one into action.

Even if it is of the second type, the emotion and depth of feeling generated, either good or bad, positive or negative, is usually unique, even if one has experienced other tumultuous relationships. The relationship to which we initially referred will be different because of the deep spiritual connection that goes with it. It will provide a telepathic knowingness of the other one and generate emotions deeper than any so far experienced. We said that on meeting this man she will instinctively recognise him at a deep level of her being. This knowledge will come from the many lives they have shared together previously."

THIRDS AS AN EXPLANATION

I would now like to consider some examples of thirds other than partner relationships. Thirds do not only impact this way. We have discovered thirds in roles as friends, as teacher and pupil, master and servant, employer and employee, for example. A spiritual third can be in any guise, friend, partner, child and parent, relative, teacher, pupil, healer and patient, tormentor and tormented, perpetrator and victim, business associates, work colleagues, neighbours, siblings and so on.

It does not always follow that the meeting has a joyous outcome or that they share the unique connection that is shared by old spirit, which is the spiritual understanding and ability to know the thoughts of each other, which comes from their unique spiritual relationship and familiarity from many shared incarnations. Older spirit thirds will have a psychic connection, the knowing of one another's thoughts, the almost telepathic connection with each other, the ability to feel the other's emotion and pain as if it were there own.

For all thirds, what is certain is that they will have an impact on each other's lives, sometimes for good and sometimes not. Of course, in spiritual terms, even if those connections are ones that seem ill-fated, they are in fact successful spiritually. The next case study is such an example.

One lady enquirer was at a loss to understand the hold the family had over her husband. Her guide responded that her husband and his mother were spiritual thirds and that, unfortunately, he had experienced a difficult childhood due to the parenting of his mother. He was completely dominated by her and would turn himself inside out in order to win her approbation. Because of this, the guide said, although he has grown in age, he is still a child where she is concerned. He still seeks to look good in the eyes of his mother and so he will do things purely in the hope of being in her favour.

I have some sympathy for this lady. Whilst my situation was not exactly the same, the originating circumstances were similar in that I have experienced marriage to a partner who had been so verbally bullied in childhood by her mother (who I suspect is her third), that by the time I met her, she had lost all self-confidence and could not take straightforward decisions alone. Her lack of a nurturing relationship with her mother had meant she needed to be parented as an adult. This is not a misfortune or a criticism of anyone as the event and its consequences were intended events spiritually. We have found from other mediumship cases, that an overbearing, oppressive and bullying behaviour in a parent is, unfortunately, quite a common experience chosen in a life-plan. The "prop" may be the same, but the lesson intended can vary.

Another explanation we had involving thirds was a lady enquirer who had a special bond with her young granddaughter. This was a mutual feeling as the child showed more affection towards her than her biological mother. The guide confirmed that the lady had not planned for her soul mate to be a partner in life and she and her granddaughter are spiritual thirds.

This same child had been diagnosed as "autistic", and naturally, the grandmother wished to ask spirit about this condition. As I have previously related, and as is written by others, there are a number of older spirits now incarnating as children on Earth, who have incarnated for a particular purpose. This relates to the new spiritual cycle of the planet. I have also said, the older the spirit, the more difficult the life chosen. These older spirits have been called *"Indigo Children"* by experts who have recognised their special qualities. They are not autistic, or suffering attention deficit disorder. They have a disability that is not yet recognised by the medical profession. In addition, our schools do not have a full understanding of the condition and these special children require a deeper understanding than they are able to offer.

In reply, the positive news the guide gave to this enquirer was that the grandchild was a special child with abilities that will not surface until she is older. In time, the disability will be recognised and treatment be available. Angela, my partner, has a grandson who is similarly a special child, being described as having some signs of autism and "unable to access the curriculum" at school. He communicates with spirit often, as he is overheard having a conversation when seemingly alone. In Angela's case, they are not thirds, but it is perhaps no coincidence, the child has a grandparent who is a medium, able to recognise his spirituality and explain this to his parents, who might otherwise feel distress and anxiety because their son was not considered "normal" by others.

I now would like to describe a case study where the impact of the two incarnating thirds is not wholly for joy, even though they have chosen to be life-partners. The enquirer, Sally, had met her husband Jack in the late sixties. He had caused her heart to miss a beat when they met, and still does occasionally now. We explained to Sally, the concept of the spiritual three and she immediately recognised that this was Jack to her. The guide then confirmed that she was indeed correct, she and Jack were thirds.

At that first meeting, advised her guide, and sometimes even now, what she experiences was the inner recognition of their spiritual selves. They have shared countless lifetimes together and on their first meeting, Sally had the inner recognition of her soul mate. The plot thickened. In 1991, Jack experienced a brain aneurysm and since then, his personality has changed. Since that time Sally has found it hard to talk to him, and he accuses her of not being supportive. Moreover, Jack has made the lives of their two daughters difficult, especially the older one, having an unfeeling and exacting attitude toward them, such that their health is suffering.

The guide gave the explanation that when Sally and Jack wrote their life-plans for this incarnation they wrote this scenario into it for the spiritual growth it would bring to them. The guide, having been asked to give a frank answer, went on to say that it was planned that the personality change occasioned by the event would remain for the rest of the life. This is the major life-event for the two of them. Sally was now at a crossroads situation, wondering whether to leave Jack for her own sake and that of her daughters. There is a past life explanation to the father – daughter problem. For the moment, I wished to use it as an illustration of how thirds can bring suffering as well as bliss.

Readers of *"Why Come Back? Book Two",* may recall that one of my own past lives was of a French seaman in the fourteenth century, killed at the battle of Sluys. This naturally caused much distress to my third, my mother, in that incarnation. Loss of a third is often more deeply felt than any other loss. In my earlier books, I described my brother's tragic accident and how my sister-in-law's life has been turned upside down in the seven years since, the loss of her third meaning her emotional turmoil has been more intense.

Sylvia Browne, the well-known American psychic who specialises in past life healing, describes a case study she calls Jane in her book *"Past Lives, Future Healing"*. This involves a mother-in-law who had become so intrusive and unbearable that the marriage of the couple broke down. In regression, Jane saw herself with her mother-in-law as "friends" in the spirit dimension, planning the next incarnation together. The theme they both had agreed to help each other with before they incarnated here was "tolerance". Jane actually saw herself asking the spirit that became her mother-in-law if she could drive her crazy so she could learn to deal with it. I would say this was a clear case of threes at work, although the author may not yet be aware of this concept.

Similarly, Brian Weiss MD, the well-known American author specialising in regression therapy, writing in his book *"Mirrors of Time"*, has made oblique reference to the spiritual three, but again may not be fully aware of the concept. When asked where souls come from if there are more people now on Earth than ever before, he stated (inter alia*): "This isn't the only place where there are souls. Earth is merely one of many schools in the universe. In addition, a few patients have told me that souls can "split" and have simultaneous experiences"*. To clarify his statement, those "simultaneous experiences" will not be the same, but different aspects of unconditional love. The life-plan of one's third will not be a mirror-image, but similarities can and do occasionally occur, as the plans of Angela and myself show.

I would now like to relate a final case study involving that of a third, one that had returned to spirit, who had a message for the one behind. The enquirer's name was Lionel and his father, who was named Richard, had died of a brain tumour at a relatively young age. Lionel had been close to his father and missed him dearly, which were possible clues to their being thirds. The message was in the form of one of Angela's "spiritual letters", where the guide, whose name was Harold, speaks direct to the enquirer. Lionel had previously consulted Angela for past life mediumship, and so knew something of his past lives. Spirit will not usually discuss extraterrestrial (ET) lives, but did so in this instance, making the message a bonus.

"My dear Lionel

I am most grateful to our friends for allowing me this opportunity to speak to you directly. It is a rare privilege, and one that is not often available, so we are fortunate to have it.

It will come as no surprise to you to know that you, Richard and I are spiritual thirds. The emotion engendered in you when you think of your father is of an intensity and depth that is usually only felt between thirds. I know you will be comforted with the fact that your father had success in his life-plan. He had in his plan, to experience the illness that he did, and although it was traumatic on an earthly level, he did in fact achieve great success through it spiritually. As your third, he has shared many lives with you, many lives with me and, of course, we have shared many lives together. We have all experienced lives on Earth and elsewhere too.

As your father is your third, this means that he will remain in spirit with me until it is your time to rejoin us. We will then be together again to review this life that you and your father have experienced and to plan the next incarnation and decide which two of the three of us will incarnate next time and where.

Your father is often with you and you feel him, we know that you do. When you feel that cobweb on the face feeling, or the breeze when there is no breeze; the feeling of something having brushed through your hair, that is him. He tries to communicate with you and such is your bond, that in time you will be able to hear him quite clearly. You often think that you do now, and yes, you do. Have the confidence to reply clearly and more will come. If you try, you will feel the love he surrounds you with, feel it like a cushion of warmth and gentleness.

Now that has explained why you feel so strongly about your father, we will discuss some of the lives you have shared with him. The last life you both shared was what you term an ET life. Life on the planet concerned is a much shorter affair than on Earth, lasting only an average of thirty of your years. The lives accomplish much in that time, however, and are lives of harmony and accord. You and Richard were the equivalent of brothers in that incarnation, incarnating and departing the life at the same time. It occurred at approximately 1799 to 1820 in your years, which was shorter than the average, and fitted in between two earthly incarnations. The one we shared when you were my father,

our last shared incarnation and a life that you shared with
Richard in which you were a Welsh miner. In that life, your father
was again your father, and worked in the mine with you. He was
one of the four who died with you in the mine.

You have had other incarnations we have not told you about,
but most of them are very early incarnations, or lives elsewhere.
We do not usually go into detail of what you call ET lives, but I
would like to tell you of one particular life, as it is one in which you
and Richard were strongly involved.

In that life, you were again in the role of the equivalent of
parent and child, but in that life, the roles were reversed. You, the
parent, were supposed to go away to take up a position that was
what you would term a promotion. It would have been an honour
for the family, but it would have meant long periods of separation
from your child, (your father in this life). You refused the position.
Your child (your father), felt always the depth of his parent's love
and regard for him, given that he was chosen above personal
advancement, and this forged a bond between you.

A life that forged a strong bond and reflected in this current life
too, was an early BC life in which you were again the parent and
Richard the daughter this time. In that life, you developed a
terminal illness and left Richard behind at a young age. You used
this plot again this time, but in a different format. It has
reinforced the lessons of love for the two of you, the love of a son
bereft of a much loved parent, and the love of a parent who knows
he must leave his much loved child.

We do not wish to go further into past lives this evening, as you
are aware of the majority of the ones that have shaped your
interests and destiny in this current life. What we do wish to do is
to send to you our combined love; to tell you how proud we are of
you, the man you have become; how pleased we are that you are in
touch with your spiritual side. We both hold you in the highest
regard, feel the deepest and strongest love for you. This is why you
feel emotion when we are around you. We both surround you with
our emotion, and you pick it up and feel it too. Richard sends you
his love, Lionel, and wants you to know that he is immensely proud
of you as your earthly father as well as your spiritual third. He
wishes you to be aware of opportunities to broaden your spiritual
involvement in the near future and he wishes you to be happy.

*My love to you, Lionel
Harold"*

I would like to thank Lionel, for allowing me to publish this very personal message. The letter is hopefully a beam of light to show the bond between thirds, which continues after so-called death and shows, when returned to spirit before us, how the third looks over us along with the guide. The letter also illustrates some of the varying roles thirds play including parental role reversal.

Among the people we have met for mediumship, have been daughters who felt a compulsion to parent their mothers because of past life roles. We have also witnessed what we feel are gender role reversals, but due to the confidentiality code, I cannot ask questions and confirm this without the persons involved actually asking the question themselves, which is unlikely, of course, because they are unable to view the situation in the same way as can an outsider. In these observed cases the wife is the dominant personality in the marriage, taking all the major decisions, the husband the submissive one, often the subject of personal insult from her as well as being ordered to do domestic chores. When a spirit that is usually male has a female incarnation, which all do at some time, or vice versa, this gender reversal might provide an interesting spiritual explanation for the social phenomenon of "hen pecking".

I would like to clarify the statement in Harold's message, that "illness", which was in fact a brain tumour, was a "great success spiritually". This may seem nonsense in human terms, but nearly all illness has a predestined quality and will be a feature of the life for the spiritual growth that can be derived from it. I devote chapter five to a discussion of illness from the spiritual perspective.

Lionel's letter from Harold illustrates the duality concept associated with life-plans. The last life spoken of, referred to Richard being left a bereaved child. In the current life, Lionel was bereaved by his father's premature demise. The lives were several thousand years apart, but that is not significant in spiritual terms. It is just that all aspects of the syllabus must be experienced at some point. Reference to "plot" of terminal illness in this letter shows it is impossible to write of spiritual threes without referring to life-plans. In the next chapter therefore, I discuss the topic of life-plans in areas not included in my first two books, in particular how a plan is written and how to identify it in the life. I also give more illustrations of this "duality principle" in life-planning.

CONCLUSION

The concept of the spiritual three is, in modern times, an entirely new explanation for certain human relationship experiences and a key piece of the understanding of the jigsaw that is the spiritual journey on Earth. On other higher evolved worlds, knowledge of the three I am told is commonplace; it is not revealed on a nursery planet, but Earth is destined to lose that status soon.

I am told that this information has not been given to me alone, but mine is the privileged task of writing about the concept and publishing it. In this, I follow the blueprint of a single older spirit being given the honour of advancing knowledge at the place of incarnation. Others will follow me to promulgate it and to enlarge upon it.

Everyone on the planet will be affected in some profound way by interaction, either briefly or over the longer term, with their spiritual brother or sister, their fellow incarnated third. It is the spiritual explanation for so much. It accords with the popular notion of a "soul mate" and so already has a pre-existing degree of familiarity and acceptance. It is one important reason for the particular significance given to the number three in spiritual matters. It gives the phenomenon of "spirit guide" a precise definition, one which was previously absent. It is the base knowledge for understanding the spiritual journey, reincarnation, life-plan formulation and review. Just as DNA is the building code material for physical life, so the concept of the three is the foundation for spiritual understanding and growth.

In this chapter, I have given examples of how human emotions and interaction can be better understood once we have knowledge of the three. Some instances of thirds as an explanation I have touched upon were:

- The search for a soul-mate; the inner knowing that there is someone uniquely close to us.

- The person that either sweeps you off your feet, or that causes you profound agony (or both).
- The uncanny ability some couples have to know each others thoughts and moods instinctively.
- The strong bonds that can exist between two family members, two friends and so on, unlike any other association.
- The antagonism or antipathy between two people causing distress to one of them.
- Gender role reversal in couples and parent / child role reversal.

I am sure there are other instances besides these, some of which might be revealed in our future mediumship cases. Thirds, of course, may not always be the explanation for the above; sometimes it can be the familiarity as members of the same soul group, having had a number of shared incarnations that produces these situations. In chapter three I give further examples using the lives of ten famous Britons, of how the third has exerted its influence on the life path, sometimes briefly, sometimes long-term but always hugely significant in the shaping of destiny. Now that I have hopefully explicated the concept of spirit threes, our biological and social relationships may be given a new understanding and perspective.

CHAPTER TWO

LIFE-PLANS

If there were no life-plan, there would be no life! It is as simple
and as stark as that. In my talks about life-plans, I use the
analogy of someone starting a new business. They will often need
finance and so approach a bank. The manager asks "Can I see
your business plan?" without which, he will not lend. There needs
to be a plan in place for each life beforehand, which includes the
major players, plots, circumstances and intended spiritual growth
for that life before an incarnation takes place.

We suffer temporary amnesia on incarnation and because of
this, we usually have no recollection of writing our life-plan. The
sources and the causes of every event may seem entirely concealed
from us. My aim is to reveal something of what is concealed by
amnesia at birth but restored to us on return to spirit. I have
therefore put together below, a table of the decision process in
arriving at a life-plan. I then go on to discuss how we might
identify our own life-plan, or at least spot clues. As usual, I then
give illustrations from our mediumship cases of life-plan
explanation for situations and circumstances.

For those whose lives have taken sudden dramatic turns, they
may well feel in the words of John Lennon, that *"life is what
happens to you when you're busy making other plans"*, but that is
not so. Unbeknown to nearly all of us, life is largely mapped out
beforehand, as regards the main events, and the detail is filled in
by the spirit guides as the life unfolds.

> *"There's a divinity that shapes our ends,
> Rough – hew them how we will"*

said Shakespeare in *"Hamlet"*. Our lives are not a hotchpotch of
random events, but a carefully scripted plan, a little like a stage
play, with actors and actresses making their entrances and exits,

plots and subplots to be included, and contingency plans arranged in case an actor forgets his or her lines. The spiritual third remaining in spirit will then act as "prompt" and "director" while his other two thirds incarnate onto life's stage to act out their play and learn the lessons planned for the spiritual progression of the three.

When planning the next life, therefore, the spirit three will need to consider and decide on several issues in order to create a successful and worthwhile life-plan. The plans of the two thirds who are to incarnate next, need to be planned in conjunction with each other, so that the required meeting takes place and contingencies can be built in if the first opportunities are missed. All three parts of the spirit three will be involved in the planning and we think it would go a little like this:

THE PLANNING PROCESS

1. Decide if the last incarnation was a success or if all or part of it requires repeating.

2. Decide if the main reason for the incarnation, the "main plot" as we have termed it, was successfully achieved and were any subplots missed that require inclusion in subsequent life-plans.

3. Refer to the syllabus of stages and levels for experiences appropriate for the particular stage one has reached.

4. Determine whether experiences require a nursery or a higher-level world. Earth is a nursery world, but different lessons are available in other, higher evolved worlds.

5. Select new main plot from a list of choices still to be accomplished.

6. Look at examples of how the choices have been put into settings by others in the past for the world of the incarnation.

7. Make a decision on how to achieve the required experiences; are any "props" you have used before of use to you this time?

8. Build in a crossroads, or indeed, several crossroads and arrange re-scripts and contingencies in case wrong choices are made on reaching them.

9. Look at what subplots need to be covered from a list of choices.

10. Build in a crossroads and re-scripts for wrong choices in these subplot matters too.

11. Select parents by looking at plans of those spirits already incarnated to find ones that match and complement your own.

12. Decide on the number of children and the broad outline of their life-plans, especially if lessons are to be learned particularly by interaction with one's children.

13. Choose pets, either new or familiar ones.

14. Select intended career, or indeed lack of it, and decide on hobbies or lack of them.

15. Look at the major events in the plan for the planet of incarnation and see if they would usefully serve as a setting for a point to be covered in your own play.

16. If incarnating on a nursery world or other lower level world, unless already decided in the selection process so far, select any major illnesses or accident that might assist your learning curve.

17. Look at the plans of others for the cluster of familiar souls you often incarnate with and decide between you if there is to be interaction between any of you. If so, build this into the plan too.

18. Look at the plan for any protégé and ensure there are opportunities to meet built into both plans.

19. Decide on what spiritual tasks need to be in the plan appropriate to stage and level.

20. Play the plan through in the Room of Destiny, so to be sure that it fulfils your requirements.

This list is naturally a little exaggerated. There are no real lists to refer to in spirit, no research is required, no one consulted as such, as all is known by all spirit. This does, however, serve well as an illustration of the concepts covered by the writing of a life-plan.

The list may be perplexing if the reader is not familiar with my books one and two. As a refresher and for new readers, I repeat the "story so far". Each life-plan will have one "major plot". If that is not achieved, then a repeat life is required. There is no punishment or judgement for a failure, and no limit to the number of repeats possible. The main plot will be designed to allow the experience of some aspect of the complex phenomenon I have termed "unconditional love". It is only through experience that we can advance spiritually. **Our progress in the spirit dimension depends on how experienced we are and all spirit has an urge to progress and return to source. It is not a question of knowing what unconditional love is, but the experiencing of it, which is the reason for the spiritual journey.**

Besides the main plot, there will be one or several "subplots". Again, these are designed to teach us about love, but the failure to experience one of them will not cause a repeat incarnation. In every incarnation on Earth, a spirit has an agenda that includes one major plot for the life and several minor plots. Failure in the major plot will almost certainly demand a repeat-life; failure in a minor one, not necessarily so, as it may be incorporated in a future life containing a new major plot. It is not always permissible that one know the major plot for an incarnation, or indeed, even the minor ones. If this were known, where would be the growth when one came to a crossroads choice? One would know irrefutably which route to take and so be denied the growth that the choice occasions.

A life-plan will not be as easy as a straight route from A to B. We intentionally build points of decision, or "crossroads" situations into the plan. One decision between alternatives will be the spiritually correct one, but there are no "wrong" decisions, only a delay process because we plan for "wrong" decisions being made. This is what I refer to as "contingency plans", where the choice is offered again to make the decision leading to an intended destiny. The making of the correct decision is part of our spiritual growth as is the endurance of the consequences, which can often be painful in human terms!

What is difficult for us to realise once incarnated, is that in spirit, one plans for things that will lead to growth. The things planned may be painful to experience in the incarnated state, physically or emotionally painful. But the experiences actually can be a success in spiritual terms because of what they teach. For instance, a bad marriage can lead to much heartache for the participants; they can view its eventual end as a failure. In fact, in spiritual terms, it can have represented a huge success because of growth, the knowledge of self and ultimately, the knowledge of love gained from the experience. We need to remember that a negative teaches by very comparison, the nature of a positive.

These may seem unfeeling sentiments. Along with many others, I have been through the emotional tortures and agonies of the end of a marriage. This philosophy may be cold comfort at the time but one hopefully can see the "you cannot obtain gold without smelting ore" analogy, with the benefit of a healing amount of time since the trauma. There is not just light at the end of the tunnel, there is the golden glow of spiritual growth; what the heart sees as failure, the soul may see as the triumph of an experience suffered but leading to the accruing of much spiritual knowledge.

DUALITY

An important principle behind a life-plan, particularly if one is an older spirit, is what I have termed the "duality principle". This is the fact that we must experience both sides of the coin to fully understand a particular aspect of unconditional love. One must experience hot in order to know cold, the opposite of love to know what love is. In order to validate one experience, one needs to experience the opposite.

This principle helps to explain why we have contrasting lives. For example, one may be a street urchin in one life, lacking everything and dying at a young age. This may well be in contrast to an affluent life when one could have all that money could buy. Similarly, a life where a child suffers emotional and / or physical abuse at the hand of a parent may be in contrast at some point to another where strong parental love and nurturing is experienced. One might experience a life in which over confidence is suffered, another in which a lack of it is experienced. One may have a life in which one has great beauty but fails to access any spirituality and conversely, live a life where one has a disfiguring illness and so learn true beauty is beauty of the soul.

Another writer's interpretation of duality is that it allows for the ability to escape it. Whilst many have observed the obvious polarities of good and evil, health and illness, there is a belief by some that there might somehow be a magic formula, a devotional escape card, a mind-set adjustment, to keep one clear of harsh experiences. I regret I cannot offer support to this view. I am told each of us must experience everything on the journey to becoming a spiritual master.

Speaking of a "devotional escape card", I watched a TV documentary about a Buddhist who walked two thousand kilometres to Lhasa, doing a prostration every three steps. It took him two years. Part of his reasoning for undertaking this monumental physical task, was to atone for the perceived wrong deeds of his father, as well as seeking his own enlightenment. Readers of my second book may recall the story of one of my own past lives, my taking a vow to make one hundred and twenty thousand statues of Buddha to show my devotion and strengthen my spirituality. In that life, I failed to see how completely unnecessary was the task I had set myself . This was the same lesson as the man on his pilgrimage to Lhasa, but using a different prop. Of course, from the duality aspect, to do something of no benefit to anyone may be a foil to a life where one advances knowledge or science to the great benefit of many or simply enhances the life of another.

Another misunderstanding of this duality is the attributing of painful experiences to "karma". This is easily understandable but again, my information is that duality happens because comparison is a great teacher about love and so the need to experience the opposite, to know some facet of love. We can have lives as a perpetrator of pain and lives as a victim of it; lives of being master then of being slave; lives as a giver of parental love and then as a recipient of it and so on. Many different and varied lives all concerned with some aspect of "unconditional love" make up the overall journey.

Another personal example of duality, readers of *"Why Come Back? Book Two",* may recall my life in ancient Greece as a Phoenician ship owner. In that life, I rejected my daughter because her terminal illness made me realise the illusory value of my wealth. In this current lifetime, one of my daughters rejected me and refused any financial assistance from me for a period of time, following my divorce from her mother. I thus have now experienced both scenarios; being the one to reject when love and support were needed most and being the rejected one, again when love and support were needed. This is not karma, although it might fit the definition used by many. In correct spiritual terms, karma is an act of unselfishness, the helping of another for no personal gain. I believe the term to have been misunderstood over time.

CASE STUDIES OF DUALITY

I should like to use some of the regression experiences of our enquirers to further illustrate this concept. To explain, a regression experience is a deep relaxation, similar to meditation, that allows access to past life memories. The person's guide reverses some of the amnesia all suffer on arrival to allow memories to appear. The following are descriptions of images of two contrasting lives chosen by the guide for a teaching purpose, as well as evidence of reincarnation:

1 **Fulfilment v Duty:** A lady had a life around the time of the birth of Christ, a most spiritual incarnation, being deeply affected by her experience. She was one of the shepherds that saw lights in the sky and followed them to the birth place. Her experience elevated her thoughts and

way of existence in that incarnation. She became one concerned with the spiritual well-being of others.

A later life she experienced was as a Geisha in the late 1500s. She was kept isolated by her Samurai owner and her only consolation was to paint. She had strong intelligence but because of her station and the social customs, was not allowed to use it. She felt imprisoned by her destiny. This incarnation was chosen by her spirit to experience exactly the emotions generated by being frustrated in one's hopes and ambitions by the need to follow one's duty. This was in contrast to the early incarnation in which she found fulfilment and was able to follow her own wishes, leading to inner peace within the life.

2 **Money v Happiness:** A lady accessed a past life memory in which she lived in Tudor England. She was a man in that life, one that was a land and property owner. In his young life, he had put the acquisition of wealth above all, neglecting his family in his single-mindedness. His wife and only son died from a fever when he was thirty-two, and he never remarried. In later years, he regretted his life and the loneliness of it and learned the lesson well.

The enquirer actually felt the emotion of the man, alone with his money and ledgers and his question, "Is this what it is all about?" She moved on in the regression experience to the time after his death. She felt the happiness and love that had not been present in the lifetime and experienced his release and the realisation that loneliness is only an earthly state.

A second life memory accessed was that of a Grecian life in Thebes around 800BC. The enquirer accessed the memory at the time of her sister's wedding in that life. She was happy to be on an extended visit to her family home for the celebrations. She also saw herself in old age in that life, the centre of a large and loving family, happy and contented with her lot. The second life was intentionally given as a counterpoint to the theme of the later Tudor one.

3 **Conqueror v Conquered:** In one regression, the enquirer saw himself as the son of a farmer who entered service as a Roman soldier. He made his life in the Roman army, fighting many battles and taking many lives. He had an inner belief, however, that this was right; that he was fighting in a just cause and had no inner deliberations. In retirement, on return to his family estates, he knew peace and contentment in old age for a life well lived.

A second regression experience was chosen by his guide as a contrast to the Roman incarnation. He saw himself walking in a Middle Eastern street in the Middle Ages, and then being tortured by Crusaders. Instead of being a soldier taking lives in the name of his country and their gods, he was the one suffering at the hands of those that were doing exactly the same, confident in their belief of their divine right to do so.

4 **Violence v Spirituality:** In regression, an enquirer saw himself as a native American holding up a child and then in conflict with mounted soldiers. He was a brave of his tribe and knew peace and contentment with his family and his way of life, which was greatly spiritual. He was forced into conflict in order to defend this way of life. This was another perspective on violence for someone who had a number of incarnations with a military theme.

A second life memory recalled was that as a Buddhist monk, a life of peace and spiritual upliftment, which was given to him to illustrate the point that the same spirit can be many things. The lesson was that violence and aggression in one incarnation, or part of it, does not preclude spiritual experience either in the same life or another.

5 **Self-imprisonment v Self-liberation:** A lady enquirer accessed memory of a life she had lived in Arizona in the late 1800s. In that life she was the daughter of a storekeeper, an only child. She lost the sight in one eye in a childhood accident which left some disfigurement to the right side of her face. Because of this and her inner issues over it, she never married, remaining alone into old age.

She felt acutely in this life, loss of love that she had not experienced, but that she herself prevented. This was an illustration of experiences within the syllabus.

In a second life she accessed an early life in Greece. In that incarnation she was, in the early part of the life, "much at sea", being spiritual in nature and wishing to pursue a life of devotion, but being offered in marriage for family reasons and family advancement. She took the decision to enter an order and, in doing so, was cut off from her family. She took the decision with a clear head and being well aware of the outcomes. She was emotionally alone in life following it, but was not unhappy; she experienced her fulfilment from following her heart rather than other people's expectations. This life, although similarly emotionally alone as in the first, was entirely opposite to it in that she was contented and fulfilled because of this, rather than tormented by it.

6 **Belief - Persecution v Fulfilment:** I use this illustration for a dual purpose. Religions and spiritual knowledge itself can be a prop for experiences. One can think of the persecution of witches, for example, who were in fact mostly healers and mediums, entirely innocent but, of course, the subject of misunderstanding, envy, projection of ill-will and the scapegoat for anyone's misfortunes. Those lives will be one side of the coin.

We have encountered several people who had an incarnation around the time of the birth of Christ. This is a fascination in itself and from a teaching aspect gives us one example of how beliefs can form a prop to one's life-plan. A lady enquirer accessed a time when she was the daughter of a senator in Rome. Her father brought a slave who had Christian beliefs into the home. Christ had died at this time, but only just. She had heard of him, which was why she had the initial curiosity that led her to talk to her slave about Christianity. This slave was, unbeknown to her at the time, her spiritual third. They became friends and she in time converted to Christianity in secret. Unfortunately, or rather as was intended to be more exact, the secret was discovered. Her father was horrified and insisted that she renounce her new-found faith. She refused point blank and for the sake of his position and political standing, he allowed her to be sent to the arena together with the slave responsible, rather than lose any standing and status.

The lesson for her father was how the one that should love and protect another, can care more for their own material comfort than for those who should be able to be confident of their care and support. His lesson was learned on return to spirit, when he was able to see how he had failed to give unconditional love to his daughter, preferring instead love of self.

The life accessed as the contrasting one for this enquirer was a life in Atlantis. There has been much speculation and writings on the subject of Atlantis. I am not permitted to disclose much, except to say it was an actual place, not myth as many believe and was inhabited by spiritually advanced people around 12000BC. We have had several enquirers who have accessed memory of Atlantean lives in regression. This particular lady was a spiritual leader in that life. Spiritual matters were the blood of life to these people, so to work in this was to be privileged. In that life, she was able to follow her beliefs openly and with joy and pride and to be fulfilled by them.

7   **Social Status v Love:** A gentleman enquirer accessed two military lives in which love was challenged by social status. In the first life, he was a knight, and in 1252, he was engaged in a jousting tournament in which he was unhorsed by the lance of another and killed. He had, in that particular life, to put the laws of chivalry, which as a knight he was pledged to uphold, above his own personal needs at an earthly level. In this life, however, he turned away from love of one with whom he would have had a mutually fulfilling relationship. The lady in question was not of high birth, and he felt the difficulty of their difference in station to the point where he failed to follow his inclinations and instead upheld the distinctions of class. On return to spirit, he realised that love is not governed by

class distinctions, and difficulties such as that are only in life to validate love by being conquered.

In the second image, he accessed a life as a World War One pilot. He was shot down in a dogfight in this incarnation, which again ended his life. In that life, he experienced the exact opposite, in that he was in a relationship with a young girl considered by others to be "much below his station". He would not give her up, however, and at the time of his demise, was in fact deliberating the fact that he was being threatened with loss of his officer status by a superior unless he acted in a manner they considered more befitting, in other words, to end his liaison.

The same enquirer had other images which were in fact, representative of an incarnation in which he was on the receiving end of the same dilemma at the hands of another. In that life, he was an actor, this was a life in the 1700s. He was the object of the affections of a lady of higher birth, who had seen him on stage. He was gifted with language, because of his occupation, and she was much enamoured. Her family, however, were horrified and she was forbidden from ever seeing him. She followed her destiny in this, however, and chose him over her family, so completing their mutual destiny.

We have noticed how some spirits tend to gravitate towards a particular theme in some of their past lives. Sometimes it can be military lives, sometimes lives as healer, leader or teacher, for example, and sometimes lives in which religion is a strong feature. We had one enquirer whose spirit had several lives exploring the world religions, including incarnations as an English village vicar, a Buddhist in China and a Rabbi in Israel. Once again the point to make is that religion is part of the cloth that holds a rich tapestry of experiences on a nursery world. **Religions are thus not to be confused with acquaintance of the workings of spirit, that I describe in this book.** They can sometimes be used as the "props" or the means whereby we experience aspects of unconditional love (faith, belief, acceptance of difference, for example), part of the syllabus of experiences that makes up the journey. Religion is part of the experiences for a race to have and work through on a planet that is in its nursery status.

These case studies remind me of Shakespeare's line, *"And one man in his time plays many parts"*. Most readers, quite reasonably, would interpret that as a reference to the events in a single lifetime, particularly as the next line written was, *"His acts being seven ages"*. This has widely been interpreted as the periods of a single lifetime. But the subliminal message or double-meaning was the reference to the spiritual journey of many incarnations by "many parts". Also, "seven ages" was a reference to either the seven stages to a level, or to the seven planes in the spiritual dimension, again another cryptic clue to the spiritual truths.

PETS AND PROTÉGÉS

I would like to further flesh out several of the points in the list of twenty, also adding some personal experience in my current life. It may be a surprise to many to hear that we chose our pets before incarnation. I would like to illustrate that.

We have a pet female black and white cat aboard our boat, the spirit of which has been our combined pet on at least five previous occasions. This explains our deep affection for her and the pet's affection for us. She has been my pet cat (male) in the current lifetime, one that was killed by a motor vehicle. She has been Angela's pet dachshund in her youth of this life. In past lives, she has been our pet cat, pet dog and pet monkey. Exceptionally for an animal, but because she is an old spirit, she has other species past life memories that show up in her behaviour patterns. The point for the moment is to say that pets will reincarnate to their owners and will have a cluster of humans they will interact with along their own spiritual journey. Pets are written into the life-plan and we may choose familiar or new ones. (I have written extensively about her in chapter six).

Secondly, I referred to "any protégé" in the list. To explain, this relates to the task of older spirit assisting younger spirit in the composition and review of their life-plans. I have become aware of two such persons whom I have so helped. The meeting of what I have termed "protégés" does not always take place, but if it does, it is helpful in the review on return to spirit. Readers may recall from *"Why Come Back? Book One"*, that level one spirits have their plans written for them by older spirits and spiritual masters. So too, do level two spirits, but they may state their preferences.

Should the older spirit decide to incarnate at the same time as their protégé, their paths may cross but on Earth both would be unaware of the situation. The younger spirit may feel drawn to the older one as a sort of mentor, or the older spirit might find an inexplicable urge to "help" the other, but neither will know why this is, due to the amnesia all experience on incarnation. Quite exceptionally, therefore, when I had encountered two of my protégés, my guide confirmed for me that this was indeed the case. It explains my unusual degree of patience in interaction with them. It also explains what others see as a most unlikely friendship, given my own character and interests. Once again, as with thirds and soul groups, spirit gives a new and surprising explanation for some of our acquaintances and friends.

CHILDREN

Turning to another aspect of the planning process, to what extent do parents know their future children's life-plans (and vice versa) before incarnation? The answer is only in the aspects that impact and enhance their own. To further explain this, if you require a child who will have mental or physical disability or early death for the lessons this will provide, then you will know that this will occur in your future child's life. If the child needs to experience rejection because of its disability, then it will know that its future parent will provide this rejection. If one is to experience jealousy at the opportunities presented to one's children for education for example, then one will know in advance that the future child will obtain its degree etc.

If the child's eventual choice of occupation has no bearing on one's own life, then this will not be known. If the choice of life partner does not affect one, then this will not be known, but if it does, then it will. If it is intended that a parent will not feature in the child's life after a certain age for some reason, then life events for either will not be known after that time, unless they are to come together again later, in which case they may be. This is one of those questions which can be answered in so many ways, but our guide believes this will give the general idea.

WRITTEN IN THE STARS

Indeed, spirit is the explanation for the whole of life's drama. Apart from acts of daily living, what to have for breakfast, what to wear and so on, there is nothing that is unplanned about the human incarnation. Things can be planned that fail to happen, but nothing happens that is not planned, apart, as I said, from acts of daily living. The fact that a freewill choice can take one off the planned path so that some planned events do not take place, could perhaps be construed as "unplanned", except that there will usually be contingency plans in place for this very happening, or the guide will execute some rapid rescripting as he or she is aware of deviations in the plan just prior to the event, so even that is planned really. Our guide went on to reconfirm this:

"I can safely say, with that qualification, that apart from acts of daily living, all is planned in the human incarnation. What is not always planned, as I have said before, is the timing or the chronology of events. Again, in some cases both time and sequence of events will be planned, but as freewill choice can intervene, this can change as contingency plans are brought into play."

I referred in the list to accidents and illnesses. How does one tell if an accident is an intended event? Accidents are the result of daily living only where there is no suffering caused, no prompting of a change in thinking, no resultant change to the previous routine of life followed for all persons affected. I should correct that, as it would be better to state "no serious suffering". An amateur football player may break his leg, which I am sure he would consider suffering, but may not be prompted by the event to change his thinking or his life routine. Of course, if that amateur footballer were to have complications which resulted in a long period of incapacity and subsequent job loss with associated financial hardships, then of course, this could also be a predestined "accident". It is hard, if not impossible to specify that this accident would be planned and this one an act of daily living, as something quite trivial to one could be quite major to another.

My "test" to determine which one, involves looking at what followed the event.

"Peace, the charm's wound up!" confided Shakespeare, a possible comfort for those who may worry over their future. It is a sentiment repeated in many popular songs, *"Que Sera"*, for example. We are given spiritual messages often; we just do not recognise them most of the time. A destiny is intended to be fulfilled, however, so we cannot be couch potatoes and expect success.

STARRING ROLES

At first thought, one might expect many spirits would wish to be someone famous and a leader, for example, a King or a Prime Minister, and so there would be a "queue" for such roles. Our guide answered that this is not the case.

"In answer to this, I would first say that there is little to be gained from being a King or Prime Minister today that cannot be gained in other lowlier incarnations. Most in these roles, are the figure-heads of a group of people, and do not have the sort of autonomy they had in your history. That said, I do appreciate the thrust of the question.

First, change the way in which you view the lessons these spirits are looking to learn. In the case of a King or any member of a royal family, they may possibly be looking to learn humility in the face of prestige; they may wish to learn that the privilege of birth brings with it responsibilities; they may wish to learn the difference between adoration of the masses and true love; they may wish to learn that love is not something that is achieved by one's rank or wealth; so many different lessons here, these are only some.

In the case of a dictator, they may wish to work through the negative aspects of love, to learn that adoration or respect achieved through brutality is not real love and will quickly dissipate when one is overthrown; and so many other lessons yet again, I have listed only the more obvious ones here.

Look at the list and see that there is nothing in it that cannot be achieved through being in a lesser role. In the first on the list, humility in the face of prestige, this can be learned by being a

48

success in any field of human endeavour. The last on the list can be learned as effectively by being a school bully who is usurped by the next bully following him. There is no lesson that can be learned by being a King or Prime Minister that cannot be learned as someone else.

It is more a case of the King or Prime Minister playing a role in the lives of others, enabling them to work through the various lessons by association with this person. It is more a case of "someone has to do it", rather than there being a queue for the post! Even a major event, such as being instrumental in taking ones country to war will not have been the sole decision of one person in many cases. Even if it is, the lessons to be learned from doing this can be learned by other events in the human life. The real result of taking one's country into war is for the myriad opportunities it affords others to fulfil a part of their spiritual journey.

Being Hitler or Churchill is no more special a role in spirit than being anyone else. One is required to fill the role in the plan, and a spirit who requires certain experiences that are provided for by the role will take it. If there is one with special talent from a past life available, whose own requirements and the lessons of the role suit each other, then it may be that one who takes the role, but it is just as likely that if you have the talent from a past life, it is not necessary to have another life in which to use it. There is no rule to this in your terms.

You must understand that in spirit there is no competition for "star" roles, no one is more likely than another to be chosen for these. As there is no superiority in spirit, the same situations do not arise as they do on Earth. I have digressed slightly, you asked if how if there is only one King etc, everyone who needs the lessons this provides can have the experience. The answer is quite simply, as I said at the beginning of the answer, there is nothing that being a King or other person of importance teaches that cannot be learned in another incarnation. Think not of the fame, the power and the wealth, but what these things actually teach! The very same lessons are offered in different guises in far lowlier life-styles."

CHANGING ONE'S FATE

Mrs Thatcher famously remarked *"You cannot buck the market!"* Can one "buck" one's destiny and for the better? Are all those books and workshops on offer really deceiving us with their promises to improve our lives?

On the other hand, there are those who caution one must be careful what one wishes for, because one might just get it! We had an instance related to us of just that. A lady related that she had what she thought was a safe career with no thoughts of giving it up. At the same time, she had been to the USA to learn of a new healing technique and longed to make her career administering it to others, but was held back by the financial stability of her job. She did not quite have the courage to take the plunge. The one in charge of the course said she was blocking her destiny so she asked for help in following it. She confirmed when challenged that she really wanted to be able to follow her path. Two weeks later she was, completely without warning, made redundant! She is now able to pursue her healing on a full-time basis instead of a part-time addition to her employment. Two days after the news, she received a letter from us, at that time unknown to her, inviting her to participate in a health and psychic event we were promoting, and so realise an opportunity to expand her business.

Synchronicity seldom comes as single spies!

From my first two books and this chapter, the reader will know much about life-plans, so knows that something you desire to happen will only do so normally, if it is in your life-plan to happen. True, it may happen as a result of someone else's freewill choice, but this usually accounts for things that happen to you which you will not have desired. For instance, a person may pray for wealth, pray to win the lottery for instance, as an end to all their monetary worries. They will only win the lottery or acquire an end to their monetary worries if it was planned that they should do so, not as a result of prayer. Their plan may provide for them to win the lottery and so have an end to their problems, and to learn from this event. Their plan may be that they will struggle on for years and lift themselves out of their problems through dogged determination and so learn from that. Freewill will possibly have offered the opportunity NOT to get into the situation where they have the worries to start with, but in this instance, it would have been spiritually incorrect not to follow the route whereby you can learn from the problems. Freewill may present a route out of the problems, and to follow it might again be an incorrect choice, or following the route out of the problems may be the correct choice too.

One can be affected by the freewill decisions of others. This can include the in-the-wrong-place-at-the-wrong-time scenarios, plus having one's own plan upset by the freewill decision of another. We have witnessed an intended purchase of a business property that was in a person's plan, not proceeding because of a third party's actions.

So to return to my question, can one change one's destiny? For example, are those who have success in bringing remission in cancer cases by use of visualisation, altering their destiny? Are the many "you can change your life" proponents speaking truly or falsely? The answer is complex. First, visualisation will only work if it is in the life-plan that it should, or if events have been followed that allow the guide to script in that it should now work. However, to say that self-help enthusiasts are raising false expectations is too narrow a view of it.

In the black and white view, yes, the statement would be correct. In that view, as visualisation can only work if it is in the life-plan that it should, by getting people to practice it in the hope of improvement is raising false hope in them. However, by practising self-help technique the person is opening to the possibility that there is more to life than the scientific approach; that in my own favoured phrase, *"There are more things in Heaven and Earth, Horatio"*. It may be in the life-plan that the improvement is to come following the practice of self-help technique, and if this were not followed in case it was false hope, then the improvement would be missed!

It is much the same as healing; the guide governs it in just the same way, and if improvement is allowed, then it will be channelled. If it is not, then it won't. Most will, however, be spiritually progressed from seeking either healing or self-help. It is therefore something to be greatly encouraged, for this reason alone, if for no other. There will, of course, be those that are disillusioned by the failure of self-help or healing therapy. It may be in their life-plan to suffer this disillusionment. In short, it is correct to encourage all healing, alternative medicine and self-help. Any of these may lead to a progress of that particular spirit.

What about prayer? Prayer does not change the spiritual programme, but that is not to say prayer has no value nor that it is not intended to play its part in a life-plan. One simple definition of prayer is that action of beseeching whatever your version of God is, to grant you something that you desire to happen.

My mantras are however, "no life-plan, no life" and "nothing takes place without planning". I have previously discussed "freewill" as being the choice between pre-planned alternatives. The use of freewill will either be an incorrect or correct choice, depending on what was intended as the more spiritual decision when the life-plan was put together. What freewill will not do however is answer a prayer. If the object of the prayer were to happen, it is because it is intended that it would, not because of the prayer.

We can further complicate this already complicated example by saying that if it is planned that what was prayed for is to occur anyway, it may have been planned that it will occur because it was prayed for. This is not the same thing as a prayer being answered. I hope the reader can see the subtle but most important difference here. In short, if a prayer appears to be answered, it is because it is in the life-plan that this is what should occur and is not a result of the prayer per se.

In case I leave the reader feeling jaundiced about the value of prayer, I wish to clarify its value and record here the answer of my guide to the question, "In view of life-plans, are peace and meditation groups deluding themselves?"

The reply was, *"The fact that many reach the point of joining a group and praying or meditating for peace, signifies the growth to want this, to desire this state. They may be mistaken in their belief that the prayer will be "heard and answered", but the combined raised vibration achieved through many meditating and wishing (which is what praying really is) for peace, is what will signify the spiritual evolving of the race; signify the rise in spiritual vibration and bring your planet to the point of its evolution from nursery world.*

These groups are providing something that is most necessary in your planet's evolution; of course, it is in the individual life-plans to do this, and so fulfils the individual destinies in the process. Prayer is a form of focused meditation and raises the individual vibration in just the same way, which allows the individual to experience what is termed the 'higher self'. When enough reach this state and have experienced their higher selves, there will be great change."

This is where the events of September 11th 2001 and ones following on from it have their purpose in the greater plan. I have more to say on the topic of the planet's evolution in my next book, but for now I continue with the subject of life-plans.

LIFE-PLAN IDENTIKIT

Once we know we have a life-plan, the obvious next question is, "How can I tell what mine is?" Well we cannot know exactly what it is, but by a process of detective work, looking for clues and piecing them together, one can arrive at something that may well produce a large part of the answer. As with crime detection, this is more of a backward looking approach, not a tool for prediction, unfortunately.

From my own experiences this lifetime, and from those of mediumship enquirers, I have put together the following list of pointers:

1. **An Agonising Decision to be Made:** These are often at cross-road situations. What may appear the easier choice in human terms may not be the correct one spiritually. Pain is unfortunately, sometimes necessary for spiritual growth.

   A scenario may present itself in your life, where there are two paths you may take. Taking one route will be easier, cause less upheaval in your life and not threaten your sense of security, but deep within you feel unfulfilled by following this route. If you were to take the step of closely examining your inner feelings, you would probably find that the "benefits" of the situation are artificial; that you are not really "happy", truly happy in the depths of your being, but just opting for the comfort of familiarity. The hard part here is to be honest enough with yourself to admit this, as the alternative might mean venturing into the frightening space that exists outside of your "comfort zone".

The alternative to the easy route might shake all the foundations of your life; might take you into this scary world outside your "comfort zone"; might lead to avenues you never envisaged, but might make you feel truly alive and fulfilled for the first time in your adult life, or at least, for the first time possibly, if you had settled into a comfortable rut. The things you discover about yourself and other people from this alternative might be the catalyst to your spiritual growth in this lifetime.

2. **A Leap Into the Unknown**: Often, when writing a life-plan in spirit, we construct situations wherein the correct choice constitutes making a decision with no certainty of outcome, an "act of faith" or an inner "knowing" that leads one to make a choice which, to the casual observer, may seem completely irrational.

   An example of this might be someone in a good, steady job, but feeling trapped and unfulfilled, suddenly throwing up their security, selling their home and setting off to travel the world in the inner belief that by doing so, they will find and follow their destiny. To those who set more store by security, position and social status than inner peace and fulfilment, such an act may seem to be that of a madman, whereas it is actually that of one having regained their sanity!

3. **Involuntary Urges and Gut Feelings**: These are often the guide at work helping us in our actions and provide evidence of our inner guidance system.

   You may find yourself doing something that is completely out of character. You may realise it is, even wonder to yourself why you feel compelled to do this thing which is so out of character for you, but still, you have this compulsion to do it. The result of it will possibly catapult your life along a path it might otherwise not have taken. This is sure and definite proof of you accessing your inner knowledge of your life-plan, possibly with a discreet "push" from your guide, Mr Fixit!

   The only clue to accessing a life-plan at the time of decision, is if one experiences what may be referred to as "gut-feelings" about the decision made or to be made. If one has a strong gut-feeling that something is right at the point of decision, then it most probably is, even if at a later time it turns out to bring pain or trauma. If one has a strong gut-feeling that one has made a mistake, even if it turns out to be materially a good move, then it is still probably a mistake spiritually.

The difficulty here is that earthly perceptions of what is correct differ radically from the spiritual definition. If one takes a correct path, but that path leads to stress, financial difficulty and trauma, one will have a very hard time viewing it as correct while incarnated. These experiences need to be gone through. To circumvent them only leads to the need to experience them at some other point in the current life or in a life yet to come.

4. **Synchronicity:** otherwise known as meaningful coincidences. When spotted, they can be evidence of the guide bringing the plan to fruition by putting opportunities in your way.

   You may meet someone by chance, who in turn introduces you to someone else, who tells you about something that changes your outlook on life. You may be in a shop and a book practically falls off the shelf into your hands. The book starts you on a whole new train of thought and interest, but the synchronicity is that if something else unexpected had not occurred, you would never have been in that shop in the first place. These are examples of synchronicity. It is true to say that if circumstances leading to an event seem too improbable, too "stage managed" to be true, then there is every chance this is life-plan and your guide at work.

5. **Illness and Serious Accident:** Serious illness is almost always something of an intended event rather than a misfortune. We write illness into our life-plan for the spiritual lessons learned from it. The lessons may be for yourself or for others in your circle, but both illness and accident provide a wealth of learning experiences for all

concerned. There is a saying, "You attract to yourself the disease you need", and it is a truism!

It is possible to get caught up in someone else's accident by being in the wrong place at the wrong time, so it is not so easy to identify if an accident is part of your plan. Sometimes the circumstances may point the way for you, for instance, if there is only one person involved, it is fairly obvious the accident was intended for them.

6. **Sleeplessness:** What we term as "worry" may result in inability to sleep. Often this is indecision about something that we manage to keep in check during our daily life, but that manages to force itself to the forefront of our thoughts at exactly the time we wish to sleep.

Often, just coming to a decision can settle the problem. Whether or not it is the correct decision will be played out in the fullness of time, but the sure and certain way to conquer the problem is to make a decision and follow it. The sleeplessness is often a guide's way of letting you know you are not on track and need to make a move. Once a move is made, it will stop.

7. **Red Herrings:** These are probably the best example of how we weave complicated webs for ourselves, when we write our life-plans. When we arrive at a crossroads situation, there will obviously be two or more routes which we could take, and in all probability, more than one will have advantages to it. Only one will be the true spiritual path, however, with the other paths that appear advantageous being red herrings. The trick to spotting a red herring is first to listen to what your inner self is telling you, and second, to look further ahead. Do not be lured by the immediate advantages, but look long term. This often points the true path for you.

8. **Dreams:** These are a common form of spirit communication. If we remember a particular dream vividly, it may contain a message of where you need to make a change within your life. The message may be couched within a dream that at first seems completely

unrelated, but if the memory of the dream is strong, or even more so if it is a recurring dream, then there is every possibility you are accessing, in the dream state, information that is excluded from your conscious mind.

9. **Opposition:** You may have a firm intention or ambition, but find a series of obstacles in your way. This is a difficult one to decipher. The obstacles may be there through synchronicity, to try and prevent you taking a wrong decision, or on the other hand, they may be there to test your resolve to follow your inner knowledge of your destiny. Spiritually, a goal achieved has much more meaning if it is achieved in the face of opposition. If you have a deep inner feeling that you should do this thing, and follow your instincts in the face of opposition and obstacle, you are likely to be following your destiny.

10. **Inner Knowledge:** Already touched on in several of the above points. Some, especially children and teenagers, just "know" where their careers lay. If questioned, they would not be able to explain how they know, they just do! This is without parental guidance or encouragement, but just an inner knowing, an accessing of their destiny.

    A natural talent that is to provide a livelihood may sometimes reinforce this. The artist Enigma always knew from a young age that he would be a popular musician. This was far more than the average teenage boy dream of being a pop star, he knew in every fibre that this was his destiny. This was to the complete horror of his mother, as he came from a family where such a thing was unthinkable. In the face of all opposition, he stood firm and followed his destiny.

11. **Visiting Mediums:** Sometimes a plan is written to include this as part of alerting the self to the existence of a certain destiny. Visiting a medium may help one view with clarity the path ahead, or even set out a variety of paths, but in a way that makes the choices easier to evaluate. It may be that the visit to the medium is the growth required,

just that. Not actual action based on messages received, but an opening to the spiritual dimension.

12. **Intense Emotional Experiences**: The scenarios I often quote for this, are those of being involved in a war or natural disaster. Both war and natural disaster are known in advance in the spirit dimension. This enables those who wish to use these events as props to achieve their life lesson to incorporate them into their life-plans. If then, you find yourself caught up in such an event, it is most likely it was your destiny to be so. It is not the event itself which is important, but the range of emotions resulting from the exposure to the event. Civil war, when families as well as nations, can be divided and split apart, adds another layer of intensity of emotion.

13. **Incompatibility of Those in Immediate Circle**: If you feel like the proverbial round peg in a square hole around your family or friends, if you feel that for all you have in common with them that you might as well be on a different planet, if you find difficulty comprehending their thought patterns and actions, then it is most likely that you wrote this for yourself, for one of several reasons, but often simply for the challenges provided by such a situation.

14. **Compatibility of Those in Immediate Circle**: There may be one within your circle that you feel close to, drawn to inexplicably more than any other person. This person may be the bringer of joy to your life, or equally, their arrival in your life may be a portent for disaster.

    This may be an indication of a spiritual Third. Thirds are not always the love of one's life; they can be cast in the role of villain too. When you hear of a couple who cannot live with each other, but cannot live without each other either, this is often an indication of Thirds. If your Third occupies a role of love, care or compassion in your life, then you are indeed fortunate in Earthly terms, as this has the ability to produce a love like no other, either the love between partners, parent and child, friends, siblings or any other combination.

This list is not intended to be exhaustive. There are no fixed rules of when subplots and main plots will occur in a lifetime, just that they will occur. Timescales are impossible to pinpoint, much to one's frustration at times. Fortunately or unfortunately, we do not receive all our surprises at once, and the interval between crossroad points can seem inordinately long at times. For example, there was five years between my divorce (one intended crossroads) and meeting my third (the next one). That is not to say there was no synchronicity, however, in between.

It is naturally difficult for us to see the bigger picture, but I am aware from my own experiences and those of others, that episodes or periods of our life can be the building blocks to a main plot. So, for example, we may develop a talent or interest in an area, undertake a period of study, have a work or business experience, that seems to lead us to no particular point, but later on, when the main plot arises, these experiences all come together and make us better prepared for the task we had set ourselves.

Sometimes our moods can indicate when we are on or off course with our life-plan. I have mentioned sleeplessness as a possible indication. We had a lady enquirer who, unusually for her, was feeling negative for reasons she could not identify. The answer was that she was failing to access her life-path. Her guide went on to say her feeling was similar to the oppressive atmosphere before the storm breaks (not that she has a stormy route), but just like the feeling that follows any storm, she will again feel the freshness and purpose of spirit. He said her present time represents a time of blind faith, not easy for anyone, but a time when all that can be done is to wait for the path to unfold.

Conversely, we have a friend who is very adept at spotting instances of synchronicity. *"I'm just sitting on my toboggan enjoying the ride,"* he said. The pop star Freddie Mercury sang that he was, *"Taking a ride with destiny, willing to play my part"*. Destiny will unfold; the variable is whether we spot it as such. For example, we may feel a person destined to have a famous life was exposed by chance or coincidence to conflict that leads on to glory but it would be spiritually more accurate to say, "his destiny was in danger of being missed until his guide got him back on track!" That final contretemps with an employer that girds the loins to go self-employed, that further expression of differences with a spouse that breaks the camel's back of wanting to hold together the relationship, and so on; these may be the conflict situations that prompt the tide of destiny to turn from ebb to flow.

MEDIUMSHIP

Let us discuss short-cutting the detective work and the seeking out of an oracle. It is one of the ethics of spirit communication not to let us know in advance areas of our life-plans, where the knowing might negate the growth that comes from freewill choices. The fact one receives no unpleasant news through mediumship, does not necessarily mean none is in store for us! It is also necessary to realise that what spirit considers to be "a correct choice or path" will be correct for the spiritual growth it provides. This does not always correspond to our earthly vision of "correct", which we would interpret as the most comfortable, most materially successful and least traumatic choice. I have had reports of mediumship where the enquirer has been given extremely unsettling information about their future path; information that is at odds with the point they have reached in their life journey. I consider such information must have had a large element of human interpretation put on it, and was not a verbatim transcription of what a guide had tried to communicate, as it is my understanding that the guide would not reveal such details until the time was right to do so.

If you seek and are given **spiritual guidance** for your future, it should be emphasised that you have freewill choice to either follow the guidance or not. Rather than being given clear guidance, you are more likely to be presented with a list of choices; your guide will possibly spell out the various avenues open to you with the positive and negative aspects attached to each, so that you may see clearly your options, but still achieve the growth from making the decision yourself.

It should also be noted here, that if you are given guidance and told that this is the correct path to follow spiritually, this does not mean it will be the easiest path in earthly terms. What is correct for your spiritual destiny and growth, may feel anything but correct when it is experienced in the incarnation! Where you are at a crossroads path, your guide is likely to outline all the choices, the positives and negatives of each choice and may, very occasionally, if the crossroads is of great importance to the life, even recommend one route over another, but will always emphasise that the choice is yours.

When asked if it is correct to do a certain thing in your life, spirit guides can only answer spiritually, that it is or is not correct to do this. They cannot forewarn you that in doing something, you will bring pain and distress upon yourself or others, as if they were to do so, their incarnated thirds would most likely avoid the path and in so doing, fail to learn the lesson that the event is intended to teach.

How does one reconcile not being allowed to know one's plan and the many acts of clairvoyance? It is because choices have already been taken, so no "secrets" are revealed. In cases where assistance for the future is given, freewill choice is always stressed, or at least, should be in instances of genuine mediumship. In these cases, however, the guidance given and the seeking of it will have been part of the plan. There is a subtlety here if we can see it; the seeking of the guidance and the acceptance of it is the means to spiritual growth in many cases, so by giving "future" information the guides are not "cheating", but in fact, achieving the plan. The next step from there is for the recipient to make correct choices having received the knowledge. The guide's answers are not always crystal clear and while they may say something is spiritually correct, following it in earthly terms may be difficult.

NOTES OF CAUTION

Some additional points to make about my life-plan identikit are:

1   **To watch out for tests of faith:** These more aptly apply to older spirit than younger spirit. These are a complication beyond red herrings. Having successfully navigated past those, one can set for oneself a test. For example, you may have chosen a new direction in your life such as to work spiritually for the benefit of others. A calamity may befall you causing you to reconsider if the decision was a correct one. I give some examples at the end of the chapter.

2 **To realise the importance of seeing destiny for oneself:** To elaborate, for some parts of a life-plan (especially those involving working spiritually in some way) it is important the individual arrives at the plan for his or herself. This is so that some spiritual growth is achieved from identifying a destiny by oneself, which can be as much as following it once you see it. We have noticed this where a destiny involved working with earth energies, healing and working with "special" children. In such cases, the guides had given hints, but also emphasised freewill choice.

3 **That care is needed once it is realised a crossroads is reached:** When an agonising decision needs to be made, which is my primary clue for a crossroads situation, it is not enough to carefully weigh the pros and cons of each path, but one is intended also to choose the spiritual route. Sometimes, ironically, the spiritual route in spiritual terms is not necessarily the obvious one. That is, what may be considered to be "spiritual" in earthly terms, for example, self sacrifice and support to one's own detriment, may not always be the spiritual route in spiritual terms. Paradoxically it might be the case that leaving a partner of many years in circumstances where the spiritual choice might seem to be to remain, is in fact, the correct one. The freedom of spirit and improvement in emotional circumstances that can come about by leaving could, in some scenarios, be the correct choice, even if financial insecurity is the result also.

As a generalisation, if an event or circumstance in life has given rise to an intensity of emotion, anger, fear, frustration, despair then it is likely this was intended to be so, to lead you to have experiences that will teach you some aspect of love. This has been summarised as, **"you need the human pain to obtain the spiritual gain!"** Growth can come from joyful experiences too, but more often it is the negative ones we experience.

I have a mantra which is, "a change of perspective alters everything!" If the reader feels that they have had test after test in this life, then do not despair. Whilst it is difficult to feel this way, the chances are that from a spiritual perspective, your life has been a huge success. If one is an older spirit, then an incarnation on Earth was never going to be easy!

I am told only a minority of our incarnations in fact are here. It is possibly difficult to accept that we have incarnations elsewhere because of almost no evidence and the fact our culture, as yet, is quite dismissive of the existence of more evolved life in the universe, although our scientists are often accepting of the possibility. The evidence I can offer is to say that in meditations and in past life regressions one's guide will sometimes allow memories of life elsewhere to surface. One of the reasons for spiritual reticence to do this, is that life elsewhere often bears little resemblance to life here. Accompanying mediumship is probably essential for that reason also, to explain the unusual images seen.

THE SYLLABUS

The guides do sometimes explain a difficult human life as being the contrast or foil for gentle and harmonious experiences in incarnations elsewhere. Working through the syllabus is the need to have contrasting experiences. As I have written, the requirement is to experience conflict and harmony, light and dark, extremes of one in order to better know the other. This is not much consolation at the time, but we should see our life from the greater perspective of the spiritual journey, not just a single lifetime. Again, it is likely meditation and regression experiences are essential in order to do this because of temporary amnesia on incarnation.

This theme of contrast can occur also within a life-plan. A illustration of this is to be found in the explanation of why we sometimes spend part of our life with those with whom we share little in common and appear to be a misfit. When you have spent time in a wilderness, spent time with those who do not think as you or seem to have any connectedness with you, it is even more pointed and obvious when you find those that do. You are drawn a graphic map of which way to go in your life, illustrated by the fact that you feel more connected and completed by these people in comparison to others that have gone before.

In time to come, I believe someone will write in detail about the stages and levels, exactly what experiences are required for each stage, to fully describe the syllabus. I also believe someone will write a thesis on "unconditional love" and explain the many facets of love. For the moment, I am only able to relate aspects of the syllabus through discovering them through mediumship enquirers. Some light is better than all darkness, so I must be content with these limited illustrations on the topic of life-plans from my case histories.

Before turning to those, let us recap the teachings given to me: We all incarnate to aid our spiritual journey and the reason for the journey is, in simple terms, to learn unconditional love. We know what this is when we are in spirit, but knowledge of it alone is not enough. We need to experience this knowledge. Each life we live adds to our store of experienced knowledge so that we may progress and eventually rejoin the Collective and enrich it by our gift of experienced knowledge. Unconditional love is not really a fully descriptive term for this that we need to experience, but it is as near as we can come within the confines of our language.

There are many different aspects of love to experience in our journey. These include: consideration of the feelings of others and of oneself, understanding of the frailties of the human condition; caring and compassion for others and for oneself; trust and acceptance, encouragement of others and validation of them and oneself. It is necessary to experience a whole list of emotions that go towards making up what we term unconditional love. I repeat here a shortened version of the list that I give on page 132 of *"Why Come Back? Book One"*: **Compassion, sympathy, empathy, kindness, consideration, respect, admiration, esteem, support, approval, understanding, perception, encouragement, trust, self-respect, care, concern, education, tolerance, forbearance, patience, charity, reason, acceptance of difference, faith, belief, conviction, approbation, appreciation, peace, harmony, amity, delight in prosperity.**

If I were to attempt to define the spiritual journey, it would be not only the experience of feeling these emotions, but also the experience of the absence of them in oneself and others; the practising of them as giver and as recipient; the experience of the opposite of them to fully know what they are, as comparison is a great teacher. On our many journeys to learn about love, we experience both the positive and negative aspects of it. In order to fully appreciate any aspect of anything it is necessary to understand the opposite to form a frame of reference. A negative teaches by very comparison the nature of a positive. To give an example in simple terms, having food does not teach about hunger, being without food does. Knowing hunger also teaches what it is to have hunger satiated.

Although these can be experienced in all stages and levels, the intensity of the experience seems to have direct relation to spiritual age. Young spirits are not tasked with such great incarnation challenges as older spirits. If you see two people with completely contrasting lives, but having the same parents or similar backgrounds, spirit level and life-plan may well explain the difference. Older spirit, I have noticed, are often tasked to work for the good of others. This can be indirectly as well as directly. Developing more understanding and tolerance of lower level spirit is also a task for older spirit. Trauma can be the means of great spiritual growth for all levels. The experience of difficulties and learning the nature of others through it, are often what we plan in coming here.

Here are some of our mediumship cases to illustrate life-plans. Life-plans are as unique as we all are, although very often great similarities can be seen.

HEALING

The first one concerns a lady in mid-life, who had a great deal of spiritual awareness and knowledge. She was a Reiki healer but felt her destiny lay elsewhere. Her guide advised her that she had chosen in this life, to assist others with her healing gifts again.

"In doing so, the gain for her own personal growth is to reach atonement with her own spirituality. The next step in the plan is to widen her scope, to become more active in her healing, more visible. She has a great gift, she should use it for as many as is possible for her. In this way, she will fulfil her destiny or her contract. She has a history of successes with the healing arts. She should only seek to realise her own reticence and she will go forward with her chosen path."

65

I repeat here a statement included in book two, which was given to this particular enquirer by her guide, which summarises the meaning of life:

"The spiritual journey for all is the acquiring of unconditional love. This is not a reference to love, as you know it in the physical, but the state of the soul when in spirit; pure and unconditional. It is the aim of all to reach this state whilst in the incarnated form. This is not achieved until one reaches the stage of true spiritual master on the earth plane, but may be strived towards in each incarnation. Being aware of the reason for existence is a huge step in one's growth and sharing one's gifts unconditionally with others is the next."

LOW SELF-ESTEEM

An enquirer suffered from this, resulting in an eating disorder such that her eating habits were in control of her and not the other way around. This was to the point she herself described as "self-destructive behaviour". She asked her guide for advice, which was received as follows:

"Glenda will easily identify those aspects she has chosen to experience in this life by her problem with her eating disorder, which she has already identified as self-destructive behaviour. From this she is learning quite graphically the frailties of the human condition; she is learning about self-esteem by the lack of it. She is learning the need for tolerance and forbearance by her need of it in others. She is learning about compassion and support by her need again, for it from others.

Her goal for the incarnation is to rise above the problem and see herself as the kind and generous person she is. To see that she has within herself the qualities she seeks in others and to understand that she should value herself on those grounds. Her self-destruction is caused by her failure to recognise her own gifts and to validate herself on those grounds. This is part one of the problem.

Part two is to be realised from a different angle, that which caused her to use weight gain and eating disorder as a 'tool' to fulfil her challenge this time. She had a past life in Pakistan in which she suffered death from starvation. In this life, she was born to poor parents, but loving and nurturing ones. Her mother herself suffered death by starvation, seeking to give whatever came her way to her four children. Glenda, the eldest daughter of the family, saw it as her destiny to continue, for her younger siblings, what her mother had done, the result being her own death from the same fate. In this life, she unconsciously seeks to redress the balance, by a fixation with food. She is subconsciously afraid of starvation, of that terrible gnawing hunger. She has developed her fixation with food as a result.

Now, let us draw the complete picture. Glenda decided in her life this time to use her eating disorder as the tool to fulfil her destiny. She needed a catalyst to make her create her current situation. She chose to bring through her distant memory of the starvation so that at an unconscious level, she would seek to compensate for it. This was one way. She reinforced this, made sure that it would take root, by choosing the scenario she described as a baby. One in which she only woke for food, so only experienced physical contact and, in her perceptions, love, in the form of food.

She created a situation in which she sees food as comforting, uses it as a substitute for love. In this, she has fulfilled one lesson by comparison and lack within herself. She has, by doing so, created for herself an appearance, a physical frame that gives her the low self-esteem and self-derision she experiences. She has created an addiction that is teaching her from the negative viewpoint, much of what I listed above."

Her guide did not leave her there in mid-air, but went on to give advice on how to deal with the situation. What a fascinating explanation for a person with a huge over-weight problem. Not diet, not biology, her life-plan is the explanation combined with a past life influence.

It has been gratifying that we have been able to give psychotherapy from a spiritual perspective to a number of enquirers besides Glenda. Conventional counselling does not at present recognise the fact that life-plans exist, and that there is no better source of information than a person's spirit guide. It is to be hoped this may change in the future. As we saw, there was an instance in Glenda's case of an intentional past life memory included in her life-plan. I devote chapter four to a discussion of past life influences on our characters.

ARRANGED MARRIAGE CULTURE

This was chosen as the prop or tool for a brother and sister we encountered. Although second generation British, their family adhered to the Eastern traditions in many ways, including that of arranged marriages. Both experienced intense family pressure to be married, and their mother felt it incumbent upon her to seek potential partners for each child, and indeed, had done so but to no avail and to the mutual unhappiness of all concerned.

The guides confirmed that the correct course of action for both the adult son and adult daughter was to wait for their destined partners and to recognise these partners themselves, which may be found outside of any arranged marriage situation. This was their life-plan and so the correct path. It was acceptable for the mother to assist by attempting to arrange marriages, but she could not be told by spirit where to look for the correct one, as this would upset destiny if it were known in advance that a certain person was the correct one.

Part of each child's test this time is to identify their partner when they meet or hear of them. The test the daughter set herself this time was to be in a community where she received pressure to marry, but to resist in the firm belief she would find her spiritual partner. This makes the position within the home difficult for both children but, advised the guide, this is really the way it should be.

For someone in unhappy circumstances, to be told "it's in your life-plan" is little comfort, and none whatsoever, if one cannot accept the concept of a pre-planned destiny. This enquirer, although she had sought mediumship and been given a timescale in answer to when she might meet her intended partner, had a great difficulty in accepting the spiritual reasoning for her situation. There is a "health warning" for enquirers; do not expect to hear the answer you want and be prepared to put in some work yourself to understand your situation. The same lady did not accept responsibility for her own destiny and sought to get others to make decisions for her. That is definitely not the spiritual route.

RELATIONSHIPS

As the proverb has it, *"Hanging and wiving goes by destiny,"* but
life-plans are more encompassing than just those events, of course.
A lady enquirer found herself divorced and away from her roots, so
naturally she sought some guidance on her future. Some people
go through a process of self analysis following divorce; some
minutely analyse where the relationship went wrong, what might
have prevented its failure, attributing fault possibly, and so on.
Some have the higher perception to see their marriage collapse as
destiny. Here is her guide's answer:

*"She has followed her life-plan with unerring accuracy to this
point. She is quite correct in that her life with her husband was in
her plan; it succeeded in bringing her to Scotland, and assisted her
with her personal growth just as was intended. She achieved a
new level of understanding in the years leading up to the final
break, and this enabled her to find the inner strength to take
matters in hand, and set the future for the two of them. She again
followed her inner understanding of her destiny.*

*It is intended that she stay in Scotland for the immediate
future; there are aspects of her life-plan that will play themselves
out here and it is right for her to remain here so that this may
occur. She will not stay in Scotland for the rest of her days,
however; the time will be when a move is correct. This will not be
to the area of her family, or determined by her job, but by the
requirements of her life-partner. It is intended that this will
involve a move abroad.*

*In the matter of career, for now, she is in exactly the right job.
This will change in due course, again with the meeting of her life-
partner, but will always be a role of instruction of others in her
own skills. Janet will find with the meeting of her life-partner,
that her spiritual progression takes a leap; this will be an influence
in her career in due course. She should be happy in her current
situation for now, however, and go along with the flow in where it
will lead her. She was right to refuse the move to London, however.
She has in her plan to attract male friends, but is correct in feeling
that casual encounters are not for her. She would not feel happy or
comfortable with this and should not attempt to fill any void in
this way."*

This same enquirer gave an illustration of what I have earlier termed a "red-herring". She had met a certain man, but it had not lasted. She asked if he was to reappear in her life. Her guide had these words of counsel:

"He is not her intended partner; she has not met him yet. Tom will attempt to surface in her life, seeking her out after trouble in his own relationship. However, it is not the relationship for Janet. Even if he is free, she would be well advised to stay clear of this as it would lead her off the track of her own destiny. Her attraction for him was arranged to create the required test of destiny."

Another enquirer sought advice about her situation. Sometimes a marriage goes through a turbulent phase. This may or may not be spiritually intended. Here is what spirit had to say about the relationship which provides another illustration of a past life influence in a life-plan.

"It is true they both 'knew' each other. Without recognising it, they understood each other because of a connection in a past incarnation. They shared an incarnation in which they had a business connection and held a wariness from that which the wife recognised at a deeper level. She will have an uneasy time in the future within her marriage, although this is some way off yet. This is as she planned for herself. The marriage will survive and be stronger for it, but she will require some support at that time, which is where her sister can be a source of strength. The sister should not worry. On an earthly level, all will be well after this short period of unease and on a spiritual level, it is exactly what is planned."

A final case history under this topic shows more of the complicated web we weave. An enquirer asked if she would be married. Her guide answered that she has it in her life-plan, to meet and then marry quite quickly, her partner. Almost, some will say without having time to know him, but she will feel as if she has known him for years.

He went on to say that the partner that she has at the moment is not the one she is destined to share her life with. This is not the correct one for her. It was not wrong that she mended the broken relationship when she did. This added another aspect to her life and decisions. It may be that now, when she is having second thoughts, the fact that she was the instigator of repairing the relationship, may have prevented her from breaking it up again; a feeling of responsibility preventing her. However, it is correct that she do this. This is not the relationship she planned to be the fulfilling and "major" one of her life this time. It was written in to her plan to serve a purpose and that is now served.

She went on to ask if a certain person she had met was her partner. The answer was that she should have no doubt in this matter. Her own feelings in this should be sufficient proof for her. Yes, this is the intended partner for her. There are several issues to be worked through here; all may go smoothly or because of the others involved there may be delay, but eventually they will be together as they both planned. He has felt the same attraction, but it often takes longer for the recognition to dawn in the male, when spiritual destinies meet (as my own personal example shows when thirds are involved).

A SEA OF TROUBLES

A lady enquirer had a most difficult life. One of her children suffered a disability from birth and had a shortened life-expectancy. Her husband had died when aged forty-seven leaving her with four daughters to raise. She began a café business and worked long hours to support her children. She naturally wished to know the reasons for her trials and whether a tranquil sea was attainable. Here is her guide's answers, which illustrate several elements of the definition of unconditional love I gave earlier. The lady I shall call Mary, and her daughter Davina. She asked about her daughter's condition, and why she was left a widow.

"Davina is a higher level spirit, who chose for herself a difficult journey this time. She chose Mary for her mother, for the depth of compassion and commitment she would give. Mary has more than adequately provided for this daughter's needs, physically and spiritually. She should not reproach herself in any way; all is as intended and although difficult to grasp on the earthly level, the incarnation is successful for Davina.

Mary will be on the earth plane to look after Davina for as long as she requires it, so she need have no concern in that area. As she knows, life expectancy is shortened, but it would be incorrect of us to give the time scale. Mary should be heartened to know when that time comes, that she has succeeded in assisting Davina to achieve what it is that soul required in this lifetime, and the spirit that is Davina is grateful to her for it.

It was Mary's destiny this time to have the difficulties she has had from facing the care of her daughters without their father to assist. The struggles she has had to balance business and family have taught her much about love and compassion, the need for balance and the nature of people. Had she had the support of her husband throughout this, the girl's father, things would have been quite different at times, so again, this is not really an area for lament, although on an earthly level it has been hard.

Mary has followed her life-plan quite closely. She has succeeded at all the major challenges to date. Now, having successfully negotiated most of her life struggles, life is intended to be easier for her in the years that follow. If we take an approximate time of four years, as near as we can say, to enable certain events to occur, she can then look forward to a gentle time in her life. A time in which to reap the rewards of her struggles and to enjoy again the love and support of another. After years of being the provider of all things, she can take time to enjoy being a recipient. Her daughters will follow their own destinies, and these will intertwine with Mary's from time to time, but on the whole, she can happily let them follow their own paths and give time to herself at last."

TESTS OF FAITH

One may need to watch out for these in identifying a life-plan. Tests of faith add complication and difficulty to the life-plan. They provide an uncertainty of outcome to the game of life, but contribute to a sense of accomplishment when successfully negotiated, when the life is reviewed back in spirit.

They are quite varied in their guises. Here is a selection we discovered:

1 **Near death experience:** This must be one of the most black and white situations, with no opportunity for

changing one's mind! Here is how one lady's guide explained her near death experience:

"In her life-plan, she wrote this for herself as part of her challenge. It was to appear that the way forward was to leave her earthly life, was to feel as if this was what spirit wanted of her, to make the challenge greater. The correct route for her, and we are pleased to say, the one she instinctively chose, was to return and so face the major part of her life's lesson for the incarnation. Until that time, she had been progressing towards the period of her life in which most of her spiritual lessons would be experienced. Had she chosen to leave, she would have missed it and would have needed to repeat this life. Choosing as she did, she has now experienced much of what she planned to and passed one of the major tests by making the decision she did."

2 **Short, serious illness:** This case study is an illustration of an illness being instrumental in leading to a pathway one may not otherwise have found, and being used as a crossroads point in a life-plan, a test of one's spirituality. In this enquirer's case, the illness took place in 1995. That was of significance in itself, and for anyone who experienced a tumultuous period that year the spiritual explanation received may be of interest.

   1995 was a year which was chosen to cause those higher evolved spirits to push forward with their spiritual journey, if such a push was required. It was the year both Angie and myself finally took the step to end our own unsatisfactory relationships; it was the year of this enquirer's long-term relationship ending and it was also the year chosen for the experience of this illness for him. These "wake up years" occur every seven years, so 2002 was the most recent at the time of writing.

   The enquirer would be able to realise that the major evidence of belief in any topic is one's own willingness to stake something of importance on that belief. As a mundane example of this, the real belief in the ability of a company to increase the value of its shares, may lead one to invest more that one could easily afford to lose. In this far more important scenario, the enquirer had chosen to leave conventional medicine and devote his life to treating sufferers by another means, effectively having no belief in conventional medicine and choosing to follow a spiritual route. What better way to confirm his own belief, than for his own life to hinge on his choosing to follow his own doctrine.

The enquirer fell ill with a fever in 1995. He identified correctly, that if he had started to perform the natural tasks indicated by his medical training, he would have indeed found himself to be seriously ill, and that the correct route to a cure was to follow the treatment he advocated to others. By recognising the crossroads, he was able to identify this and avoid the pitfall. In effect, he passed the test of trusting his own health, something of extreme value to him, to his own beliefs.

The fact that he correctly identified this as a position of choice, also confirmed his spiritual ability to continue in his chosen field of medicine. The period of unexplained ill health following the crisis forty-eight hours in his life, gave him this opportunity to think clearly, to recognise that death held no fear for him and to emerge from it as a different person. This was indeed a major crossroads, and the year provided many of a similar spiritual level with similar opportunity to pursue the destiny they had planned in spirit.

3 **A calamity**: I use our personal experience of this, so write in some detail. As readers of my previous books may know, my partner and I live on a converted wooden Scottish fishing boat. On 26th June 2002, I was standing in a harbour bottom, which had dried out at low tide, to repaint the underside of the boat, which weighs some sixty tons, and when out of water is approaching the height of a house. A third party came along and caused the boat to fall over whilst I was scraping off old paint. I had to leap for my life out of the way and Angela, who was inside the boat at the time, was thrown violently from one side of the cabin to the other, closely followed by a just-boiled kettle! For some minutes she believed me killed, but I had just beforehand,

moved from the middle section where she had last seen me, to the bow of the boat, and thus had been able to leap clear.

This was a near death experience; not in the psychic sense, but on the human level of coming close to death, escaping it seemingly miraculously, but then undergoing shock and trauma of the experience. I am sure many in wartime, will have had a similar one.

The experience included a certain numbness of senses in the aftermath, a profound sense of disorientation, a need to talk through the circumstances with any willing listener, feeling the need to punish the person who caused the incident, having a sudden distaste for the lifestyle previously cherished because that very lifestyle had given rise to the incident, a questioning of spirit for the causes and reasons why, a rejection of the spiritual path and looking at a return to a more material life, these were some of the emotions felt.

A week or so of thinking over the incident had resulted in the conclusion it was not an intended event, that it was a case of being in the wrong place at the wrong time, that there was no obvious spiritual benefit for us. Because we were already spiritually aware, this was not a wake-up call.

The question of whether it was a test was dismissed because where was the choice? We had none at the point of the experience, but to suffer it. Angela did say the choice came afterwards, whether to continue on a spiritual path or not. I dismissed that, having only briefly considered the alternative, but remaining steadfast in my conviction we work for the spiritual growth of others, even if so far they were very few in number.

Then I took a phone call from a friend. "Doesn't it make you want to give up, after all you are doing for spirit?" That was it; pennies started dropping. Angela and I both agreed it was a test, not an act of daily living or a wrong-time wrong-place situation. It could not be a scenario of daily living as we had both been traumatised by it. I pointed out the older spiritually one is the more one is tested out, having some historical examples in mind in saying that.

We discussed the "engineering" of the event. How the local boatyard owner had said he could not take us, then changed his mind after the accident, but in the first instance, causing us to use the drying out grid. How at 10am on the fateful day I had telephoned the nearest boatyard some fifty miles away asking to book their slip, and decided to leave on the next high tide. Along came the instigator of the accident at 11am whilst the tide was still out. Neither of us had been seriously physically hurt, quite remarkable in itself. In a few days, we found satisfactory accommodation on land, allowing us space to recover our equilibrium. Yes, the pennies were indeed falling.

As proof, we both felt an immediate lifting of spirits in having arrived at the correct diagnosis by ourselves, having as it were, earned a congratulatory pat on the head. I am not sure if this was our soul recognising an intended trial or the guide rewarding us, but either way, we felt much happier and now able to put the experience behind us.

We recognised we had now achieved the purpose of our being at this place. I coined the phrase, "We're only here for the accident!" (not the beer, and laughed.) That explained why we had not practised mediumship or developed spiritual contacts here. Another clue uncovered in support of the diagnosis.

Of course, I recognise that to put the spiritual explanation to a non-spiritual person would result in him or her concluding I had been concussed and was having difficulty in seeing the world "rationally". To the average person it was an accident, the result of an act of stupidity accepted, but still not the acting out of some pre-planned event in spirit, and brought about by spirit guides pulling the strings of human puppets. That stretches credulity, is too "off the wall" to be real, yet it is the truth.

The spiritual test for us was the main purpose behind the "accident" but there are others to come. Our guide naturally would not elaborate on them, wanting us to spot them for ourselves, but I suspect they will include:

1. The opportunity for spiritual growth in the person who caused the event. His employers may take action causing him to be affected in the longer term. He may suffer guilt and much internal questioning.

2. Our using the experience as a teaching aid, to show how
    we set challenges for ourselves, crossroad points of
    allowing freewill to come into play, as tests of
    spirituality.

3. Our own world-view altered. What seems most
    important at times (financial security for instance,
    which had been occupying our thoughts and concerns) is
    in fact unimportant, having experienced the possibility
    of fatal or very serious injury.

4. Our using the experience also to relate the
    "synchronicity" of events both before, during and after
    the accident, that reveal the guides at work.

5. The connection of trauma with soured earth energies.
    The town suffers from this, caused by a history of coal
    mining in the locality.

6. Absent healing, and the use of colour and sound in
    healing, as friends sent us their support.

7. As a further test of our spirituality, not allowing
    ourselves to be angry or vengeful towards the person
    who caused our distress, nor towards the guide, the real
    "eminence grise" or instigator, knowing this was life-
    plan in operation.

8. My increased communication, brought about by the
    ambience in the lounge of the rented flat. (We later
    discovered it was built on an earth energy "spring").

If there is suffering, there is a spiritual purpose. This is
how I now distinguish between what is an intended event
and what is not. What we plan for ourselves in spirit
seems masochistic at times, difficult for the human mind to
comprehend. As I have remarked, a change of perspective·
alters everything, so does the experience!

KEEPING TRACK

One final point is to consider the "Akashic records" that some writers describe as being the record of all of our past lives. We had an enquirer who had been told that there is a huge gap in his Akashic records. This was a reference to the fact that he had an abhorrence of violence, aggression and strongly held dogmatic views. There was a past life explanation for these feelings, which Angela gave to him. In planning subsequent lives, he tried to avoid violence or brutality. This is unusual said his guide to take those feelings back to some degree into spirit. On return to spirit, he is privy to all past lives and the reasons behind them, and so should really understand that lives containing these aspects are necessary too, for growth and advancement. He should realise the need for these lives and not try to avoid them.

The guides went on to say that what is termed the Akashic record is more a human concept, one used to explain the gap in experience such as the one just described. There is no real keeping of records; souls are responsible for their own progression. If they miss areas, it hinders their eventual return to the Collective, the thing that all spirit strives for. In this way, it is self-regulating, there is no need to keep score or write a report, they confirmed.

CONCLUSION

I expect few of us enjoy the thought that we are puppets on spiritual strings, but that is one view of our pre-planned lives. We do write the script beforehand, where choices are made but the choices are from a prescribed list. Our incarnation consists of illusory attributes when we think we create our own destiny, exercise unfettered freewill, think as we like, form relationships with whom we choose, and so on. On the other hand it may be a great comfort to know that there is a design to life and we are not like air-borne seed at the mercy of the winds of change, that human suffering does have a purpose.

I cannot demonstrate the amnesia I am told takes place on incarnation, but life-plans can be inferred from the many instances where someone has an inner knowing of their destiny, has an immediate recognition of people, occupation, or a place that "feels right" for their life. There are many instances of our guide at work if we stop and consider, that we can detect as synchronicity, gut feelings, dreams and so on. These are the clues to the engineering that takes place to make our lives pan out the way they do. Having been previously roughly sketched, the fine lines to the life-plan are added later by the guide once the show is "on air".

The reader can perhaps undertake a little exercise using my life-plan identikit to see if they can fathom their life-plan to date. Alternatively, one could make a list during a period of quiet contemplation using an emotional barometer to detect life-plan. If one noted all the highs and lows and the events or circumstances associated with them, together with the subsequent feelings and events that the initial highs and lows gave rise to, then this may reveal aspects of life-plan. It is difficult to be accurate without enquiry of spirit, but there is one profound overall realisation that can be made; what has happened in life to date was more than likely what was intended to happen. It may be readily apparent or it may be difficult to spot, but there will be a spiritual purpose to those events. The painful consequences of "the slings and arrows of outrageous fortune" are what gives rise to much spiritual growth. If there have been blows, these will not have been misfortune but intended events.

I now leave my general discussion of life-plans and look at the lives of famous individuals to illustrate the life-planning that underpins and overlays our lives.

CHAPTER THREE

GREAT BRITONS

Having discussed something of the process of composing a life-plan, and some clues on how to identify the plan, what might illustrate graphically the concept is to look at some famous lives through a prism of detection to suggest what their plans might have comprised.

The BBC in late 2002 broadcast a television series *"Great Britons"*. The public was invited to vote for the greatest-ever Briton, and from that a list of the one hundred favourites was produced. For each of the top ten nominations, the BBC commissioned a one-hour film, each with a different presenter as the advocate. The public was able to vote either by telephone or "on-line" via the internet, after each programme to determine the final position of those in the top ten.

My choice of famous lives for analysis is the top ten as voted for in this television series. The winner was Winston Churchill, followed by Isambard Kingdom Brunel. The other eight were: Elizabeth I, William Shakespeare, Oliver Cromwell, Isaac Newton, Horatio Nelson, Charles Darwin, John Lennon and Diana, Princess of Wales. I do not intend to breach any confidentiality, as my factual sources are the published biographies for each. The interpretation of the lives is, however, from the spirit dimension. (All is known in spirit; when in the spirit state, it is possible to know the past lives of any spirit and the intended experiences).

There is a contrast to be made between "greatness" from a human and from a spiritual perspective. It is not an easy word to define, but some of the human qualities associated with greatness might be: enterprise, talent, intellect, wealth, courage, notoriety, popularity, power, impact, originality. If a single word were used it might be "achievement", which would be outward achievement, rather than inner achievement, which is where greatness of spirit lies.

Greatness has a very different definition in spiritual terms although modern biography has been said to let in daylight upon the magic of public heroes. From a spiritual perspective, illumination is the knowledge that we each have a life-plan and have spiritual guidance to help it come to fruition; that one life is but one of many and so too limited a time span for comparison purposes. In any event, in spirit there is no ranking by greatness or any other yardstick, merely progression for all through a syllabus of experiences. There is no scoring or grading of a life, just a pass or fail.

Silver Birch, the bringer of spiritual philosophy in the 1920s and 1930s, has commented that the heroes in our world are not those of the spirit dimension. He comments on the countless host that serve others with no desire to be known or recognised. He would consider the criterion of what message a soul has left to guide others as more important than the popularity or notoriety achieved by the individual.

Three out of the top ten have lives strongly linked with conflict. Our culture honours courage on a battlefield, but who is to say that is any more laudable than the courage of a cancer sufferer? It is the inner battles of the mind where spiritual greatness is forged. I speculate that achievement in spiritual terms would be choosing a difficult life with the aim of advancing quickly through the stages and levels.

One life-plan blueprint I have found particularly interesting personally, is that of choosing shipwreck, and being part of a small group of survivors in a lifeboat far from land. As if the trauma of the experience and relief at surviving the initial disaster would not be enough, the survivors may be faced with the great stress of limited food and water. After a period they would have the stark choice between all dying a slow painful death or resorting to cannibalism. Having decided on the latter, the guilt and mental turmoil that must follow is unimaginable; far greater than the guilt of killing a stranger against one's conscience, which some have found themselves experiencing in wartime situations.

The major "prop" for a life-plan could be something as small as a lifeboat, or as big as world politics. Life-plans need to be seen in a wider context, especially when the life is one that is "famous". Jeremy Clarkson in championing his famous Briton, Isambard Kingdom Brunel, asked, "What made Britain great?" With some good reason he argued that it was our innovators and engineers. But let us look at the global picture and the plan for the planet. Seven out of ten of the most voted-for Great Britons lived in the three-century period from Henry VIII's dissolution of the monasteries (1536) to the mid-Victorian era, the Great Exhibition (1851). Is this a coincidence? Surely not, as very little happens by coincidence.

The fact that England became a world power beginning with the reign of Elizabeth I and reaching a peak in 1918 is no accidental coming together of circumstances and events. It is no fluke of history that England became the first nation to industrialise and became the powerhouse of inventions and "the workshop of the world". It was in the plan for the planet that this should happen, that Britain should be the first country to do so, to be then followed by others.

I hope to provide clues to the existence of the world-plan, to complement those of individual life-plans, in a later book. For now, let us take the most remembered event in the reign of Elizabeth I. The year 1588 saw the famous and unlikely defeat by the greatly outnumbered English of the Spanish armada. Nostradamus' prophecy number 10/100 for the year 1588 was translated as follows:

> "The great empire will be made by England
> All-powerful for more than three hundred years
> Great forces will move by sea and land
> The Portuguese will not be happy"

As with all his prophecies, he was seeing the future plan for the planet, using spiritual communication. These plans are written by Spirit Council for periods of two thousand years, which put details onto the outline formulated by the Collective.

We think of advances of science and technology and the arts as being the product of individual genius because normally one person is credited with the discovery or application. We may speculate on what precise circumstances prompted the creative moment, whether it is in music or literature, a major scientific breakthrough, the brilliant military strategy, or a daring political initiative. But from the spiritual perspective, there is no need for such speculation.

If a person brings to the planet advancement in science or the arts, it will have been in that person's life-plan to do so. He may have had an innate skill, the product of previous incarnations. He will have had the assistance of his spirit guide who knew the life-plan and all the thoughts of his incarnated counterpart. The individual may have an inner knowledge of what he or she is going to create, tapping into life-plan memory. Alternatively, the guide will lend a helping hand, giving "inspiration" when it is needed. What we describe as genius may seem to be thoughts from seemingly nowhere, but are sometimes the guide's thoughts put into the person's mind. All advances in science and the arts are pre-planned and given to individual spirit as part of their progression task.

I would like to recap and explain the sub-headings I have used in discerning the life-plans of the ten most famous Britons, before going into an analysis of their lives.

1. **Choice of Parents**: This can sometimes be a most difficult spiritual phenomenon to accept. Children choose their parents for their spiritual life-plan compatibility. In spirit it is the number of children and the various experiences one hopes to achieve through the parenting of the children that is written into the life-plan, not the exact spirit entities who will be these children. Once incarnated, it is the guide's role to "interview" and "cast" appropriate spirit that will be the children of the incarnated parents-to-be. The choice will be made based on the life-plans of both complementing each other well. Sometimes the choice of parent / children will be from the soul groups of both.

2. **Main Plot**: This is the aspect of love one has chosen to experience, failure to do so will result in a repeat life being required.

3. **Subplots**: These are other aspects of love one has chosen to experience, the failure to do so will not cause a repeat life.

4. **Crossroads**: The choice between alternatives one builds into the plan. These I have called a "test of spirituality", as one will be the more correct spiritually, the other a side-

track. They are key decision points that will have a major impact on the life-path.

5. **Inner Guidance**: These are instances of keeping on the straight and narrow of a destiny, or returning to that straight and narrow. They can vary from an inner knowledge of the life-plan, to thoughts and feelings communicated from one's spirit guide to keep one on the intended life-path. This communication is often without the person's conscious awareness of it.

6. **Synchronicity**: These are the many coincidences, often unrecognised, which show the guide at work to get one to be in the right place at the right time to achieve one's plan. This can include "bumping" into someone; a particular book "falling off" the shelf; catching or not catching the particular aeroplane, train or boat that has a disaster ending.

7. **Past Life Skills**: All genius I have written, is the tapping into abilities acquired in previous lives. Just as we may bring forward particular fears or phobias arising from experiences in past lives, so past lives can explain particular talents or "gifts".

8. **Human Faults**: Spirit in its natural state is "unconditional love". What we experience through the human body includes the faults, foibles, emotions, lack of understanding of empathy and of consideration that the human state is prone to exhibit at times.

9. **Spirituality**: All spirit in its pure state knows what unconditional love is, it just varies in the amount of experienced love that it has. In book one, I described the five levels that all spirit moves through on its journey of experiences. Earth is mainly composed of young or level one spirit, followed next by older or level five spirit, with smaller proportions of the intermediate age spirit, levels two, three and four. Level five spirits are not saints, but will not usually have the extremes in the negative emotions

and behaviour that younger spirit sometimes has (although there are always occasional exceptions for some reason or another). They will often exhibit a greater sensitivity for other's feelings and be more willing to give of themselves, service to others being the spiritual pathway.

My sources for the information on the lives of the ten greatest Britons are the book *"Great Britons"*, supplemented by information from the internet and, on occasion, a biography. From these, there is insufficient detail to deduce the complete life-plan, but sufficient to give a basic outline, supported by examples of synchronicities and subplots to illustrate these concepts. Some Britons such as Churchill and Nelson, had such colourful lives that they would have contained many examples of synchronicity.

Winston Churchill, 1874 – 1965

I have put together the following, which I consider to be the basic framework of his life-plan:

Choice of Parents:

1. Born at Blenheim Palace, his chosen family were the aristocratic Marlboroughs, with their tradition of fighting for King and country. This was important in forming values and the ambition to follow in those footsteps, in preparation for his future role.

2. His parents were also chosen for the challenge as they were both cold and distant. His self-belief had to come from within himself, not something inculcated. His father was openly critical of his seeming lack of talent and he did well not to let this blight his life.

Early Subplot:

He experienced an unhappy school life, due to being bullied. It was an opportunity for him to learn about oppressive behaviour in others, which could have influenced his actions as a politician in later life. As Home Secretary, he seemed not to have learned from this, however, as he adopted a bullying stance with others. Later, however, this same school experience shaped his resolve in resisting the oppression of Hitler at all costs. Two lessons were thus intended from one "prop", one a success and the other not.

Crossroads Examples:

1. The choice of career was an early crossroads for Churchill. He very nearly did not get into Sandhurst Military Academy, only passing (just) the entrance exams at the third attempt. A push was needed from his guide to ensure he did not give up!

2. His success as a war correspondent during the Boer War could have led him into journalism as a career. He entered politics instead, becoming a Member of Parliament in 1900.

Subplot Failures:

1. As Home Secretary, he took a hard line on law and order matters, using the army against suffragettes, trade unionists and anyone who challenged the system. An opportunity was missed to show tolerance and sympathy for others' grievances.

2. The Gallipoli campaign in 1916 was a military failure. As the main proponent, he took responsibility. He nearly lost his sanity and the event was the trigger for his first major bout of depression. He did not recognise that we each have destinies and to lead others to theirs is not a cause for guilt.

His Third:

This was his wife Clementine, chosen to take the supporting role in his life; she was clever and loyal. She helped him through his depression bouts, a subplot in his life.

Inner Guidance Examples:

1. He took himself off to the trenches of World War One. This proved the antidote to depression.

2. His repeated warnings against Hitler in the 1930s; a lone and unpopular voice against the tide of opinion. This helped to mark him out as the choice for Prime Minister when destiny finally called.

3. His outward certainty of victory despite the odds and the burden he carried as wartime Prime Minister.

4. His warning at the end of the war, about the expansionist tyranny of Communism and the Iron Curtain falling across Europe.

Human Faults:

1. He was rude and unpleasant to his staff at times.

2. He had drinking bouts and episodes of bad temper.

3. His political failures included making little attempt to improve the conditions of ordinary people.

4. He was politically backward-looking at times, a planned human fault to facilitate his role in the disastrous return to the gold standard in the late 1920s and his opposition to Dominion status for India in the 1930s, both of which were intended events.

5. He exhibited a failure to deal compassionately with others' grievances, the suffragettes and the trade unionists, for example.

Major Plot:

The man of the hour, the one needed to rally the nation, not to make any pact with Hitler, but lead millions to their destinies in taking part in World War Two.

Synchronicity Example:

After the failure of the Norway campaign and subsequent criticism, Neville Chamberlain called a meeting with Churchill and Fairfax, the two frontrunners in the event of a change of leader. Chamberlain's own preference was Fairfax, but he declined to contest the leadership saying he had a stomach complaint. This move by Fairfax allowed Churchill to step into the job they both wanted. [A guide can communicate by triggering illness or creating "gut feelings"].

Inner Knowledge Example:

He said on being appointed Prime Minister, "I felt as if I were walking with my destiny, and that all my past life had been a preparation for this hour and for this trial." His sense of destiny had also sustained him through the preceding personally difficult years.

Past Life Skills:

His past life skills included those of orator and communicator (perhaps the Roman era), which helps explain his talent in those areas, which were ones needed for the major plot.

Spirituality:

Churchill was a high level two spirit (by that I mean he was nearing the end of level two). This may come as some surprise given he came out top in the BBC poll. The human faults give some important clues to his being a relatively young spirit. His popularity is attributable more to his role, of course, than how he performed that role. World War Two was in the plan for the planet (many references to it are in the predictions of Nostradamus). Churchill has hero status as the saviour of the nation but was far from being a spiritual master. Although his was an important part, it was in a script already written. A leader's scope for influencing the course of events is really quite limited, because the outcomes are planned in advance and we, the spirit actors, are guided to reach those outcomes.

That may seem a hard to accept statement so let me give a couple of illustrations. We all know, for example, Churchill's words on the Battle of Britain result, when *"so much was owed by so many to so few"*. With the German bombing of English airfields, the RAF was losing the battle and staring defeat in the face. Then there was an unexpected change in German tactics when they began to bomb London. The airfields had time to recover, which they previously lacked. It allowed the RAF to survive and go on to victory. What prompted the change in German tactics? A single bomber, against orders, having failed to find its target, dropped its load on London. There was retaliation by Britain, and the previously adopted convention of not bombing each other's capital was torn up. A seemingly inconsequential event thus had major significance for the final outcome. That single bomber's actions would not have been by accident or happenstance, but "divine intervention".

A similar swing in the pendulum of the fortunes of war can be seen in the Battle of the Atlantic. The German U-boat campaign, Churchill confessed, was his greatest fear, threatening as it did the vital supplies from America. In March 1943, the Germans felt they were within an ace of victory, so staggeringly successful were they in the tonnage of shipping sunk. Then once again, England snatched victory from the seemingly poised jaws of defeat, with record U-boat sinkings, causing the Germans to withdraw from the Atlantic in May 1943. Military historians have said, quite correctly, it was a combination of factors that gave the Allies victory, but whence the inspiration and guidance for those tactical and technological advances that contribute to it? Germany was destined to lose the conflict and had "help" in doing so.

What is fascinating to contemplate is the fact we have given mediumship to spirits currently living as English men and women, but who had lives as Germans during World War Two. We have met the spirit of one who was at that time, a factory worker in the Ruhr valley. He was in fact killed during the famous Dambusters bombing. We have also met a German pilot shot down in the Battle of Britain, now also an Englishman. World War Two really does make no sense with this knowledge, except of course, it was the means to provide countless spirits with extremes of experience and so accelerate their spiritual growth. On a nursery world, wars are like an accelerator pedal in the vehicle of experiences along the spiritual highway, until wars become no longer necessary.

One of the most difficult questions I am asked is, "So you are saying six million Jews chose their fate?" One needs to look at that from the perspective of one of hundreds of lifetimes. Secondly, it will have been for the contrasting experiences against lives of love, peace and harmony, which will also be enjoyed by those same spirits, so yes, I am saying that. This type of experience is only found on a nursery world, but it is just as much a part of our total experiences as any other. We have to experience both sides of the coin, as I explained in the previous chapter. It is necessary to look at the emotions generated and the lessons that were learned by both the Jews and their tormentors to fully understand this perspective.

Isambard Kingdom Brunel, 1806 – 1859

From the information in the *"Great Britons"* biography summary, Brunel's life-plan would have been this:

Choice of Parents:

Clearly it made sense for someone with a destiny to be a famous engineer to choose a father, Marc Brunel, who was himself a noted French engineer. His mother was English and he was born at Portsea. His father conceived and patented machinery to make pulley-blocks and also designed a tunnelling shield which allowed a tunnel to be excavated under the Thames.

Planned Accidents:

1. Brunel nearly drowned in the second flooding of the Thames tunnel, where he had gone to work with his father. The accident occasioned his move to Bristol in 1828 for convalescence. Much of his life's work was to centre on Bristol and the accident served to get him there.

Like many spirits, prior to incarnation, he would have made a reconnoitre of the places that were to feature in his life-plan. He had decided Bristol was to be the port for some of his important projects.

2. Trying his hand at being a magician, he swallowed a coin at a children's party, which stuck in his throat and nearly killed him. This led him to invent a device to help dislodge the coin.

Major Plot:

Brunel's major plot was to be an engineering star, who tirelessly worked on projects requiring complex organisational ability; to be the creator of visionary designs, applying new engineering principles and to make leading edge projects involving tunnels, bridges, docks, ocean steam ships and railways. He quickened the pace of industrialisation and world communication, his life being part of the greater plan for the planet that this occurred.

Human Faults:

1. He was a workaholic, seldom taking holidays and readily sleeping in his office. Consequently he neglected his family by being a slave to his work. He wrote, "My profession is after all, my only fit wife."

2. He sometimes miscalculated, for example, in the power requirement for railway engines, and engines for the *"Great Eastern"* steamship.

His Third:

Because of the huge influence he must have had on him, this was his father. Their life-plans intermingled, especially through the Thames Tunnel project.

Subplot Examples:

1. The Thames Tunnel experienced serious flooding during

which Brunel rescued several men and during which he was himself injured. He could have chosen not to help.

2. To experience opposition seems the concomitant of fame. An example in Brunel's case was the criticism of the *"Great Western"* steamship from Lardner, who claimed the voyage could not be made, a view widely accepted. Her successful voyage in 1837 confounded the critics.

3. By giving his body and soul to his work to the detriment of his physical and mental health, the lesson of not ignoring self-love, the need for balance, had not been learned. He sacrificed his health in the drive to complete the *"Great Eastern"* steamship project.

Crossroads Examples:

1. He entered his father's office as assistant engineer at age seventeen. He had shown talent in several areas at school and could have made other choices.

2. His resignation as engineer in 1846 of the Great Western Railway paved the way for his talents to flourish in other areas besides railways.

Inner Knowledge of the Life-plan:

1. He had the drive to see through his projects in the face of opposition.

2. Some of his projects were too visionary for the times, for example, his atmospheric engine, which used vacuum to draw carriages along a railway. He was using knowledge acquired previously to develop the work of others.

Past Lives:

His engineering skills had been practised in previous lives elsewhere, which helps to explain his great talent.

Spirituality:

There are some clues to this in that he never took out a patent, that he was not interested in personal fortune and was willing to help others, even his professional rivals. Brunel was a high level five spirit, evidenced from his bringing new knowledge to the place of his incarnation, one of the tasks older spirit perform when they are ready to do so.

Horatio Nelson, 1758 – 1805

Like Churchill, one needs to put his life, as all lives, in the context of the plan for the planet and the fact we, as individual spirits, bring that plan to life, put colour onto the black and white outline already sketched. The heroes of the human world are not those of the spirit dimension and a heroic life of itself, is no more worthy than a nondescript one. That is not to say the individual with the heroic life may not have achieved much personal growth and no doubt he will have helped many others achieve their destiny by having a leadership role.

We ascribe victory to the skill and genius of the military leaders, yet in spirit the outcome of all wars and battles is known in advance and an individual leader's scope for affecting the intended outcome is small. I am sorry to burst the image of another hero. We are all actors on life's stage and the script of world events has been written long before our arrival. Within that script, the experiences of wars and violence are intended to be only a small part of the overall experiences each spirit will acquire on its journey from, and back to, the Collective.

Choice of Parents:

1. It was necessary to have the hunger for distinction which lay behind his maverick spirit. To be born into an aristocratic family may not have produced that drive whereas to be born into very humble origins may have been too problematic to rise above them.

2. While his origins were not humble, his family did have a lack of money, which meant all the children sought a means to fend for themselves at the earliest age.

3. He experienced some early tragedies, notably the death of his mother when he was aged nine and the death of a brother aged eleven when Nelson was eight. These experiences helped to mould his character.

4. His father was rector of four parishes in north Norfolk. Religion was a subplot in his life-plan.

5. He had an uncle, Captain Maurice Suckling, who proved most influential in Nelson's naval career.

Human Weakness:

1. His great vanity was a planned-for fault. It helped him achieve his destiny to become a hero and obtain the glory he did.

2. He could be petulant, irritable, self-promoting in the extreme. *"He is in many points a great man; in others, a baby."* (Lord Minto)

Subplot Examples:

1. Being born into a rector's family meant Christian beliefs might have served two possible purposes: to be a sustaining source in his later life as a military leader or to constitute a challenge for him to realise there was no real foundation to such beliefs. Such realisation would come on return to spirit if not in the lifetime.

2. His over-zealous application of the laws against American trading ships in the West Indies earned him unpopularity with the British admiral and the governor there. He was put on half-pay in 1787 and stayed on "garden leave" for five years. An example of a wrong decision, but one showing how the guide got him back on track later. In

1793 he was given a new command with a bigger ship. In this, he shared with Churchill the experience of having to wait, marking time, till his destiny arrived, till his main plot transpired.

Inner Guidance:

1. Even though his weak and frail physique as a twelve-year-old suggested his unsuitability, he knew from an early age that he wished to go to sea. An example of knowledge of the life-plan.

2. Recovering from a bout of fever as an eighteen-year-old, he had a vision of a "radiant orb". He felt an intense patriotism and exclaimed, "I will be a hero, and confiding in Providence, I will brave every danger." The experience gave him confidence and drive, which he never lost. (The orb would most likely have been his spirit guide).

3. His impulses to insubordinate behaviour in his career, which proved successful were often "inspired" by his guide. (An example of "Roger's involuntary urge"! This is described on page 150 in chapter seven *of "Why Come Back? Book Two"*).

His Third:

Emma Hamilton would be the choice because of the impact she had on his later life. They first met in 1793. Emma hero-worshiped Nelson, and nursed him back to health after the battle of the Nile in 1798. Their love affair scandalised many. The subsequent impact (for the worse) of their affair on both their lives, shows how meeting one's third is not always for joy alone. He recognised her link to his destiny, "my saint", he wrote to her.

Crossroads Example:

Meeting Emma Hamilton, married to an English diplomat, meant casting aside conventional Christian moral standards and a social taboo of the time.

Synchronicity Example:

His first recorded passionate love affair was with Mary Simpson, aged sixteen, whilst he was in command of the frigate *"Albemarle"* in Quebec. At the moment of weighing anchor and sailing away, Nelson took to the shore in a small boat to propose marriage, not caring if this might ruin his career. A friend spotted him and argued him out of his resolve which was an example of the guide using a third party to influence his incarnated third.

Main Plot:

To be the country's naval hero in containing Napoleon within mainland Europe; to initiate British naval supremacy for a century, facilitating the enlargement of the British Empire in Victorian times, and thereby creating circumstances for the destined huge growth in world trade for Britain.

Past Life Influences:

Before this incarnation, he had experienced careers at sea and had military lives previously. His compulsion for heroism in this life may have been a compensatory one for a failure to have acted heroically when this had been expected in an earlier incarnation (an example of an intentional past life unconscious memory).

His Wounds:

These were written into his life-plan, the loss of the right eye and loss of the right arm. They made him an even more colourful character, and enhanced his hero status.

Illness:

1. He contracted fever (malaria) in Bombay in December 1775, with such severity he was sent back to England. He suffered a deep depression followed by his "radiant orb" spiritual experience, which resulted in his, "I will be a hero," statement of destiny, showing this to be an intended illness because of the resulting insight into life-plan.

2. The West Indies station was dreaded by seamen because of
   the prevalence of the deadly fever they called "Yellow
   Jack". In 1779, Nelson's crew of two hundred officers and
   men all succumbed with the exception of ten survivors. An
   instance of terminal illness not intended for him, (but even
   so, it caused him to be invalided home).

   It is interesting for me personally to note that the ship
   on which the sick Nelson sailed from India back to London
   was *"HMS Dolphin"*. In one of my previous lives, I had
   sailed on a circumnavigation voyage on the same ship some
   years earlier. (The story of that past life is told in Chapter
   Two of *"Why Come Back? Book Two"*).

Spirituality:

His concern for the conditions of ordinary seamen may have had
ulterior motive rather than altruism, as unfit men cannot fight.
In later life he did, unsuccessfully, try and institute a pension
scheme for ex-servicemen. The published summaries of his life do
not suggest he was a person given to great introspection, with
many inner battles to fight; a level three spirit in fact.

Charles Darwin, 1809 – 1882

Darwin's life shows, as all lives do, that we do not plan to travel
from birth to death, A to B, in a straight line. We build in points
(crossroads) that can lead us off track, even take us to a different
destination if we allow it, but inner knowledge will often guide us,
as does our spirit guide, his or her influence visible in the
instances of "synchronicity".

The older the spirit, the harder the lessons, hence the
bereavements, struggle with his conscience to publish, and public
opposition to his ideas that Darwin endured and overcame to
make his life a great success spiritually. Just as I started out with
no belief in an afterlife or in the spirit dimension, so Darwin began
with the view that species are immutable, and later arrived at a
contrary opinion. A one hundred and eighty degree turn is more

difficult and profound a manoeuvre than a short course deviation! It is a challenge chosen by older spirit. Darwin's most famous remark was, "I'm almost convinced (quite contrary to the opinion I started with) that species are not (it is like confessing a murder) immutable".

Choice of Parents:

1. He came from a line of freethinkers, a natural choice for someone with his destiny. It created an environment which questioned established ideas, particularly religious ones.

2. His parents were sufficiently wealthy not to cause him to have to put livelihood before study, allowing him to go on the *"Beagle"* voyage of five years and live his subsequent life as a gentleman and independent scholar. They did provide some challenges for him, however, as his mother died when he was aged eight (an early subplot).

3. His family had strong links with that of the Wedgewoods, the wealthy industrialists. He married his cousin, Emma Wedgewood. His family, notably his sisters, provided him with emotional support.

Choice of Wife:

Not his third, but important to his own life-plan was his wife Emma. Her family's wealth was a contingency plan if Charles' father had not indulged his son. She became his rock and guardian angel. "His luck in marrying Emma was breathtaking", says his biographer Cyril Aydon, but of course, marriages are made in heaven, not chance but written into the life-plan.

Main Plot:

Darwin's main plot was to introduce new thinking contrary to creationism, thereby accelerating the wane of religion's influence on the Western mind and to exhibit the mental courage to do this. [Evolutionary theory was not new; what Darwin did was produce the evidence for it.] At his death, his influence on human thought was being compared to Newton or Copernicus, showing the success of his main plot.

Whole Life Contingency Plan:

Should Darwin have failed this main plot, then spirit had a second person with the same one, to ensure the new knowledge was introduced by one means or another. His name was Alfred Wallace, who simultaneously developed the same key concepts as Darwin. As it was, Wallace was used to prompt Darwin into going public as left to himself he may never have done so.

Contingency Planning Example:

So important was it to his life-plan to promote the science of evolution, that Darwin was given several chances to be drawn to the subject. Early ones were:

1. His grandfather, Erasmus Darwin, had written a long poem (*Zoonomia*), which contained a long section on the evolution of species. The book had been one of the most talked about in its day and was another reason for his choice of parents.

2. At Edinburgh University one of his professors, Robert Grant, espoused the theories of Jean Lamarck who, in the year of Darwin's birth, published a book on theory of evolution.

Inner Knowledge of the life-plan:

1. As a boy, Darwin had a fascination with botany, collecting beetles and reading avidly.

2. Darwin never stopped studying and working throughout his life, his search for knowledge an addiction. He had an ambition to make his own contribution to scientific knowledge, triggered by reading a book when a twenty-two year-old student, by the astronomer John Herschel.

Crossroads Example:

Darwin was sent to Edinburgh to study medicine so as to follow the family tradition. However, he was more interested in natural history, so his father sent him to Cambridge, hoping to turn him into a parson if he would not be a doctor but Darwin carried on with science.

Synchronicity Examples:

1. He witnessed two very bad operations as a student at Edinburgh, which eliminated any interest he retained in a medical career.

2. "The chance of a lifetime," writes Andrew Marr – his invitation to be unpaid naturalist aboard *"HMS Beagle"* about to begin a five-year circumnavigation. His going was not a certainty; his father initially opposed the idea. Darwin's uncle helps him change his father's mind. Two others invited came close to acceptance, but withdrew for "family reasons".

3. The ship visited the Galapagos Islands, where Darwin observed birds and animals unlike anywhere else and different on each island. Along the coast of Chile, he witnessed an earthquake, which provided him with the answers to the forces that could raise beds of seashells high above present day levels.

4. He read Malthus' *"Essays on Population"*, which gave him the insightful flash of how evolution worked (Wallace too was inspired by that same work to arrive at the same key insight.)

5. Wallace's uncanny arrival at exactly the same theory of natural selection finally pushed Darwin into publication of *"The Origin of Species"*. For twenty years he had delayed making public his explosive theory.

Example of Missed Synchronicity:

Darwin had no knowledge of how inherited characteristics were passed through the generations. It was a gap in his theories for the sceptics to pour through. Mendel's pioneering work on genetics was made public in a scientific paper in 1865, a copy of which Mendel sent to Darwin. It lay still unopened in his study the day he died.

Subplot Examples:

1. Darwin suffered greatly from the deaths of his children. (A painful lesson to be learnt is that our children are our children biologically only). The death of his favourite daughter aged ten, finally shattered his Christian beliefs. This, of course, helped him face the hostility of the Church to his ideas. One "prop", two lessons intended.

2. On the other hand, the acceptance of difference in beliefs in others, even when quite opposite to one's own, is an aspect of "unconditional love"! Darwin succeeded in this, respecting his wife Emma's sincere Christianity throughout their marriage.

Example of Life-Plan Complementing That of Another Besides Parents and One's Third:

The scientist Thomas Huxley, in contrast to Darwin, was not shy of controversy and polemics. They met in 1853 and Huxley for the next six years was a fierce proponent of evolutionary thought, preparing the ground for publication of Darwin's big concept.

Illness:

For forty years he suffered a painful and debilitating illness, with two lessons intended as with the death of his child. The first lesson was the opportunity of the bringing closer of his wife, and the second, illness acting as a brake on any inflation of ego as a result of his discoveries. (Spirit recognises this human frailty and plans for it, not always successfully as my readers may have noticed!)

His Third:

This was his friend and fellow botanist Joseph Hooker. He used him as an intellectual sounding board, respected his intellectual honesty and felt close to him. Hooker became "a co-opted assistant in Darwin's quest for the laws of life".

In this life, it is interesting to note the role of the third was not a biological one or that of life partner, but that of friend. They would have had a subconscious recognition of their spiritual connectedness, a knowingness stemming from many shared past lives.

John Cooper in *"Great Britons"* used language that approaches the concept, but is unaware of it. He describes Darwin's early trust of Hooker as "intuitively brilliant" for example and explains their forty years of intellectual and personal relationship, not without fierce disagreements, as being due to the "magnanimity of both men". Yes it was, but then as thirds, it would be!

Opposition:

As with Brunel, opposition was the accompanying side dish to fame. Many argued Darwin's idea dethroned God (the intention!) and made monkeys of men. The debate still continues in some quarters today.

Human Weakness:

I can only spot two blemishes on his life from the spiritual perspective.

1. First, his concern over his gentleman's status; he did not wish to put it at risk by publicising controversial theories. This proved an unfounded concern in the end, but was what lay behind the delay in publishing his two best works, *"The Origin of Species"* and *"The Descent of Man"*.

2. Second, he devoted an excessive amount of study to less
    important subjects, notably eight years (1846-54) on the
    lifecycle of barnacles, before work on species began. He
    later confessed, "I doubt whether the work was worth the
    consumption of so much time".

Spirituality:

An early indicator of his advanced spirituality is the fact that he
abhorred the cruelty and slavery he witnessed in South America
on his *"Beagle"* voyage. Like Brunel, he was a high level five
spirit, this fact revealed by his introduction of new knowledge.

He was also a member of Spirit Council. (Please see *"Why
Come Back? Book Two"*, Chapter Nine, for an explanation of this).
The distinction between Darwin and Brunel was the fact that
Darwin introduced knowledge that changed the way people think,
that challenged established ideas, particularly man's place in the
scheme of things, whereas Brunel although advancing science and
progress, did not do this.

Darwin was correct in his theories. What he did not know
about, and was not intended to include, was the spirit element and
life-force that each and every living thing contains. Spirit, as I
have written, introduces new knowledge on a piecemeal basis. His
deeply felt loss of his daughter Annie, may have been to him, a
demonstration of the cruel and capricious nature of existence, but
again, he was unaware of the spiritual design to human life. My
part is to show the overarching spiritual orchestration and
choreography that accompanies human and animal physical life,
to build upon Darwin's world-view change of thought.

Whilst he was correct that man's physical body was a descent
from common stocks, he was unaware of the spiritual dimension.
The great difficulty for many, the step too far, was for man to lose
his special status, which was what Darwin's theories implied. In
truth, spiritually, man does have special status. The highest
variety of spirit uses homo sapiens for experiences and first began
to do so around 10,000BC. (I describe something of my own
Neolithic life in my second book). Prior to that, the spirit that was
"early man" was the highest variety of spirit of the type that
incarnates as animal, not without some degree of intelligence, but
nothing like that of the type of spirit which we all are.

A report in the United States recently showed a minority of adults, forty-four percent, agree that humans developed from the earliest species of animals. The way to reconcile the opposing schools is to acknowledge that spirit uses homo sapiens sapiens as a vehicle for experiences. The evolutionists are not denied and the creationists have their comfort in that God has created all life, but has done so using evolution. Science is a discourse, divisive as such because it separates us from metaphysical concepts. Its original description was "natural philosophy", which is much less divisive. In the spirit dimension, there is just knowledge, an understanding of the laws which govern the universe, both physical and metaphysical.

Darwin's natural selection left no place for divine purpose, or so it seemed. He followed Gallileo in challenging the authority of the Church to explain the natural world, and by implication, its right to direct people's thinking on any matter. He succeeded admirably in his main plot. I for one, in my teenage years, used the argument that if the Church was wrong about creationism, what was it right about?

Darwin did not give the world privileged information. I am told all of us in our spirit state, have access to all knowledge of a general nature. What is not allowed is for spirit to pass on information to incarnated loved ones that breaches the need-to-know basis rule of communication for the stage of development for the place of incarnation. What Darwin did was play his part in the greater plan of the planet, whilst simultaneously achieving the experiences he required as a high level spirit.

The plan called for religion to be superseded by science as the dominant ideology in the West. This process started in England with Henry VIII's dissolution of the monasteries and gathered pace, although not before taking some extreme or fundamentalist twists (the Puritans, the Reign of Terror, for example) along the way, although those of course were planned too, for the lessons obtainable. Just as an individual life-plan is never a straight line A to B, so it is with the plan for the planet itself. In time, however, the influence of all religions will greatly shrink, to be replaced by knowledge of spirit and of the workings of spirit as the world leaves its nursery status behind.

In Darwin's personal case, the aspect of love he was required to experience through his main plot was love on its widest base, love of one's fellow man by introducing new knowledge. You may ask, "Why did spirit not give Darwin the knowledge it wanted to become public on a tablet, in the fashion of Moses?" The task for Darwin included the struggle to reach the knowledge, and then to put it together in his books, his spiritual growth coming from his achievement in doing this. There is a parallel here, very close to home as this has been my task also.

You may also ask, "Given the objective of diminishing the influence of religious ideology, why did Darwin not write about spiritual truths instead of evolution?" The answer is that it was not time to do so. Only with the new cycle for the planet that began in the year two thousand, is it the time for this. (That is why Degas (1834-1917), for example, who knew of the concept of the spiritual three, could not speak of it, but only represent it in his paintings of three dancers.)

Isaac Newton, 1642 – 1727

In view of the complexities we construct for ourselves in the life-plan, the wonder is we manage to succeed in them as much as we do. Failure rates can be as high as fifty percent on occasion (or rather, the need to repeat can be that proportion).

Newton did succeed in his main plot, but it was touch and go at times. For example, he almost blinded himself with early experiments investigating light and vision. He developed a great shyness to publish, getting embroiled in needless arguments with fellow scientists. He became greatly side-tracked with his deep interest in alchemy, numerology and theology. Finally, he showed the human frailty of choosing the material life, becoming Master of the Mint. Thankfully this was after he had published his masterpiece, but even so he had to be prompted into doing that.

Choice of Parents:

They form one of his subplots, his family difficulties being part of the challenge older spirit chooses for itself. His father died three months before he was born. His mother remarried when Newton was two, and seems largely to have abandoned him. The young child had an unhappy childhood, raised by his grandmother. He had an uncle who was a Cambridge graduate who helped steer him there.

Main Plot:

To be the founding figure of the Enlightenment movement, a movement which pushed back the stranglehold of religion on thought, ushering in the secular and industrial age; to achieve the personal spiritual growth by introducing new knowledge to the planet of incarnation.

Early Subplot Example:

He suffered an uninterested mother and no father in his life. He perhaps succumbed to these childhood difficulties in that he never married and spent much time in isolation as an adult.

Early Crossroads Example:

Had his talent not been recognised by his headmaster, he may not have reached university. His mother was unsupportive and wanted him to run the family estate and so took him away from school at the age of seventeen. However, he decided he was no farmer, so successfully negotiating a crossroads situation in his life.

Subplot - Illness:

1. Whilst not intended to affect him personally, the plague, which closed Cambridge University in 1665, enabled Newton to spend two years at home. This proved a most productive period, crowded with brilliant discoveries. The closure of the university was helpful to him also, in getting a fellowship there, because more vacancies than usual became available when it re-opened.

2. In 1678, Newton had a nervous breakdown, and had a second one in 1693. The first was a subplot for him, the experience being one chosen as part of his plan. The second

was a message for him that his life was not on track, designed to affect his thinking. Unfortunately it did not succeed in its aim (I say more in chapter five on how illness can sometimes be a message for us).

Human Weaknesses:

1. He spent a long period as Master of the Royal Mint, becoming rich and having little further interest in research. He preferred social status to science.

2. He feared criticism, or certainly had an abnormal reaction to it. His long dispute with Hooke, another scientist, caused a long delay in publishing his work on light.

3. He had a dispute with Leibnitz over whom discovered calculus first, (quite unnecessary if Newton had not been so slow to publish initially). He kept up an obsessive belief in his own uniqueness, in his being chosen, not having the generosity of spirit to see there might be another his equal.
   The intention was that they collaborate. Instead, their arguments led to a schism in mathematics between Britain and the continent that lasted generations.

4. He could fly into irrational temper, especially when criticised. He adopted a dictatorial manner as President of the Royal Society.

5. He showed some vanity in his commissioning of flattering portraits of himself, an aspect of his obsession with self-image that fuelled his disputes with other scientists.

Synchronicity Examples:

1. There is the famous story of him once being bullied by a much larger classmate, and Newton challenging him and beating him. The bully was one place above Newton in their class ratings. Newton resolved to beat him academically too and did so, rising to first place in the school, thereby coming to the headmaster's attention.

2. He bought a book on astrology in 1663 at a fair near Cambridge to see what there was in it. He could not understand the maths in it, and this triggered him to read books on maths, the start of his deep studies in that subject.

3. Similarly in 1664, he bought a prism at a fair, which led him to study light. This was from a fair at Stourbridge near Cambridge, which included stalls selling all manner of oddities.

These are two examples of seemingly inconsequential purchases which had far-reaching import for the major plot. Synchronicity is almost impossible to detect sometimes, only with hindsight is it revealed. Missed synchronicity would only be known to the guide, of course.

Opposition:

1. As with the example of Brunel, this is intended as the spur to fame and also the means to highlight it. Hooke disputed some of Newton's work on optics, which he took badly. There is vituperative correspondence between the two. They remain bitter enemies until Hooke's death in 1703.

2. Liebnitz, a contemporary German mathematician, criticised Newton's entire concept of gravity. Both developed a band of protagonists to champion their respective masters, in a rivalry lasting decades.

   As in drama, opposition in life creates tension and arouses emotions, making a plot hold one's attention. Here, through freewill choice, the opposition component of the plan had much more space that was intended because the actors "ad-libbed" and did not adhere to script.

Past Life Influence:

Newton had been a mathematician in a previous life elsewhere, which explains his brilliance once he studied maths in this incarnation.

Past Life Connection:

Newton has an uncharacteristic warmth for a much younger person, Fatio de Duillier. Their attraction was mutual. There has been speculation as to the exact nature of their relationship. He was, I believe, a son in one of Newton's past lives. He became Newton's close companion for a period. Newton's second nervous breakdown followed closely the ending of their relationship, the trigger for it but not the cause.

Inner Guidance Examples:

1. In the words of John Maynard Keynes, he had *"unusual powers of continuous concentrated introspection"*. One also might call this meditation, the explanation Newton himself used as being the means to his discoveries.
   "The notion of gravitation came into this mind," wrote William Stukely of a conversation with Newton. An example of his guide's communication, I would say, illustrating how scientific advancement is in fact, not human genius alone, but spirit directed.

2. He is driven in his search for truth. He had no recreation, spending all his time in studies. He possessed a powerful impulse for knowledge. Again, to quote Keynes, *"He regarded the universe as a cryptogram set by the Almighty"*.

Coordination of Life-Plans Example:

Newton had a band of influential disciples and interpreters – John Conduitt and John Desaguliers, for example, whose life-plans co-ordinated with his.

Subplot Failure:

Newton's interest in alchemy was a side-track as was his interest in theology. (He left behind over a million words on the subject of alchemy). He spent as much time on them as mathematics. It was intended he investigate then reject these areas. (What I have termed red herrings.) His second bout of mental illness was his guide's attempt to get him back on track.

His Third:

Not easy to spot; clearly neither of his parents, and he remained a bachelor. His third was Edmond Halley. They did not meet until 1684. Halley urged Newton to write a full treatment of his new physics, which he did (*"Principia"*). Halley personally helped to get it published. It became "the greatest scientific book ever written". The Royal Society had run out of funds to publish any new books, thus a crossroads choice was presented to Halley – his decision to use his own money.

    The meeting of one's third in this instance, as can often be the case, is shown to be instrumental in achievement of the major plot of the life-plan. Newton's dispute with Hooke had made him turn in on himself and shy away from publishing. An engineered meeting between the two thirds saves the drama from stalling.

Spiritual Level:

Newton's choice of parents shows an older spirit life-plan in its degree of difficulty. His introduction of new knowledge to the planet is the revealing clue to his being a high level five spirit.

    The poet Philip Larkin, penned his famous sentiments about parents passing on their faults to their children,

> *"They fill you with the faults they had*
> *And add some extra, just for you".*

This is one half of the classic nature / nurture debate. One biographer, Michael White, commented that Newton was damaged emotionally by his childhood experiences, but what then explains his great intelligence? His father like many of his class, could not sign his own name. Some psychology theories attribute intelligence level to a combination of genetics and upbringing, so how would Newton fit this view? I think it difficult to argue that his genius stemmed from his nurturing as he had an unhappy childhood. It is unlikely to be genetic as neither parents nor grandparents were academics. The spiritual explanation is that genius is a mark of talent acquired in past lives and a mark of spiritual age. His degree of intelligence is linked with his high spiritual level. (Readers may recall my discussion of the nature / nurture debate in chapter six of my first book).

The fact that the spirit that became Isaac Newton chose to be English was not an accident. He might easily have been European, but as Nostradamus foretold us, the plan for the planet was for England to be in the ascendancy for three centuries. As Roy Porter wrote in his book *"Enlightenment"*, *"Newton was the god who put English science on the map"*. He was the icon that was crucial to the English Enlightenment, was the mainspring in the paradigm shift that ushered in the Age of Reason. Again, this was all part of the greater plan for the planet and England in particular.

Newton fulfilled a part in the wider script. Naturally, he is credited personally with advancing knowledge and understanding, which facilitated the Industrial Revolution a century later. From the spiritual perspective, his life was a task chosen and a challenge appropriate for his spiritual age. It is in the performance of the role that we should look for greatness, if we must, as with any actor on life's stage. For the spirit that was Newton, that life was but one of hundreds, but of course, one of perhaps few on planet Earth, his being an older spirit and the Earth only being used by mainly young spirit.

Elizabeth I, 1533 – 1603

Having had one of my own past lives in England as an Elizabethan, I follow this period with some interest.

Past Lives:

Her political gifts had been honed as a leader in earlier lives. She mostly had male incarnations; this one was an exception. She was a high profile example of gender reversal, which explains some of her character traits. Her famous self-description was, *"I know I have the body of a weak and feeble woman, but I have the heart and stomach of a king".*

Main-Plot:

To continue the geo-politics begun by her father, Henry VIII, in consolidating England as a Protestant state and to begin England's period of Empire by resisting the powerful Catholic Spain.

To advance the notion of women as decision takers in a largely patriarchal world as Protestant religion had not brought any improvement in the status of women; to exhibit the personal courage and resolve to carry out the role, to show a love of self and a love of others to do this.

Subplot Examples:

1. Her brief period of imprisonment in the Tower of London at the age of twenty-one had two intended lessons: first, to teach her compassion to others, and second, to strengthen her resolve to resist the Spanish invasion in later life.

2. To resist the pressure from the male establishment to marry and produce an heir. By successfully doing so, she allowed the "spin" of "the Virgin Queen", an image which outlived her, and more importantly, she did not diminish her feminine role model by taking a husband. A tough subplot that lasted forty-five years of her life.

Human Weaknesses:

1. She had frequent attacks of nerves.

2. She lost her self-control when in love.

3. She was happy to take her share of the booty her seadogs stole from the Spaniards.

4. Her sponsorship of alchemists was perhaps a weakness; the historical equivalent of today's heavy gambling on the lottery!

Her Third:

Not easy to spot. Her love affair with Sir Robert Dudley, Earl of Leicester, might indicate past life connections. The role of the third here is to test as well as to bring joy. Had she married him, the life-plan may not have been achieved. She correctly saw that this was not the way, seeing the absence of political benefit. It also served her because having known true love it was easier for her to reject foreign suitors. This is a perfect example of the third's role in affecting thinking and promoting the life-plan of the other incarnated third.

Choice of Parents:

Elizabeth had little choice, because of her main plot, which necessitated her to have Henry VIII as a father. Her mother was in fact his second wife, Ann Boleyn. She was educated by people who favoured reformed religion and she became fluent in languages, both useful to her life-plan. She had the trauma of her mother's beheading when she was aged three, and a life of constant insecurity under the reign of her half-sister Mary.

Crossroads Example:

Elizabeth declines an offer of marriage made by Philip of Spain. Not an easy decision, but as it turned out, everything depended on the husband Elizabeth did not take! This was contrary to the opinion of the Spanish ambassador, who along with many had the view her choice of husband was critical to everything else.

Inner Guidance Examples:

1. Thomas Seymour announced his intention to marry the adolescent Elizabeth. He planned also to kidnap the boy King Edward VI. He was arrested and executed. Only by

keeping a very cool head did Elizabeth escape a similar fate. The guide, no doubt, helped in that!

2. When Edward VI dies, the succession is contested and Princess Elizabeth is summoned to court, but wisely pleads illness. It was being communicated to her that this was not the correct time.

3. Elizabeth shows an awareness of destiny, announcing at her coronation, *"I am already bound unto a husband, which is the Kingdom of England"*. Few believed her though!

4. Elizabeth selected extraordinary able and upright ministers such as William Cecil and extraordinary able, if less upright ministers, but ones dedicated to her cause, such as Francis Walsingham for example. Who assisted her in her decision? Her guide, of course!

Spirituality:

"By the standards of the day, Elizabeth was an extremely merciful monarch," writes Michael Portillo. Her agonies over death warrants, her religious tolerance and her loathing of extremism point to a higher spiritual being, level four in fact.

Elizabeth's reign saw an English renaissance, with many talented people, especially writers and musicians, living during this Golden Age. The foundations of the future British Empire can be traced back to this time (Sir Walter Raleigh's Virginia colony, for example). Elizabeth herself waged no war for conquest's sake. Her interventions were to help fellow Protestants and thereby her own country's stability. In that, she followed her main plot and succeeded admirably in her life-plan.

This outward success was her role in the wider events of her reign, which of course, had been predetermined, laid down in the plan for the planet in the cycle covering the years we refer to as 0AD to 2000AD. Her inner success was the self-love experiences of being isolated, yet still achieving and of showing a love for her people in her devotion to them. These are level four experiences which occur again in level five.

Shakespeare, 1564 – 1616

Main Plot:

England was destined to be the premier world power, and what better way to help that come to fruition than expand the English language in a way never achieved previously. (His vocabulary was 29,000 words). Not only that, to use plots that show the characters' spirits tested, and to discuss the perennial problems down the ages – issues of race, gender, money, power and its corruption – all the very stuff life-plans are made of!

In the words of Fiona Shaw, "No other writer in any language has been able to map our emotional DNA with such accuracy". I would paraphrase that and say, no other writer has been able to give us the spiritual script put onto the earthly stage as well as he did.

Human Weakness:

The fact that he used his worldly success in later life to acquire property and social status for the benefit of his family might be construed as a human weakness. However, he was in fact providing an important part of the life-plans of others in doing this.

Past Lives:

He had been a writer in many previous lives.

Whole Life Contingency Plan:

His early works did not match the artistic quality of his contemporary, Christopher Marlowe, whose life was cut short in a pub stabbing in 1593. Marlowe was intended to be Shakespeare's back-up for the main plot, if he had stumbled. He was also the catalyst that gave Shakespeare an even greater urge to succeed, by providing him with "competition". Shakespeare did not stumble, of course, and so as soon as it was obvious he would follow his life-plan, as was intended, Marlowe did not remain to be competition to Shakespeare's work, or to distract others from it and its spiritual messages.

His Third:

Marlowe, his catalyst and his back up! Their interaction with each other was much more than is recorded by history. Being of the same spiritual level, Marlowe only incarnated to support Shakespeare, but returned to "other work", once it was clear he would not be needed further. His means of doing this was for the lessons and experiences of others within his circle.

Past Life Connection Example:

Shakespeare's wife, Anne Hathaway, had shared previous lives with him and provided the background role while he had the limelight. Unusually, she was older than him when they met, which provided a minor test of spiritual recognition for her, who would normally not have considered it seemly to have a younger man as husband.

Choice of Parents:

The choice of Stratford-upon-Avon had significance from its closeness to Warwick, a site of importance in relation to earth energies. Those aided his spirit communication. His father was sensitive to earth energies and spiritual communications, so William was encouraged in this way. His family had some status in the locality, but his father's business fortunes fluctuated.

Subplot:

His only son died in 1596, aged eleven. The loss of a child teaches much about love that is not realised while the child lives, and this was an experience Shakespeare had not used in his portfolio, having chosen different means of learning the particular point. He chose to have the experience in this life although he had nothing left to achieve personally for his own spiritual growth.

Inner Guidance:

"His mind and hand went together," his publishers reported. The ease with which he wrote his masterpieces points to the help of his guide and his past life skill.

Spirituality:

Lawrence Olivier said *"Shakespeare – the nearest thing in incarnation to the eye of God"*. Closer to the truth than he would have realised perhaps in saying that, although I would prefer to say "the voice of God", Shakespeare was a Spiritual Master. His incarnation was therefore one of choice, coming back to help others, having nothing to gain for himself spiritually. Not only that, he was also a member of Spirit Council, the body responsible for overseeing the evolution of all planets, carrying out the wishes of the Collective.

It is not therefore surprising he could give so much insight into the human condition and his plays contain so much information about spirit; his communication with his guide was of the highest order. His incarnation followed Nostradamus, another Council Member (1503-66). Both lives had a similar purpose, to deepen spiritual knowledge in those who recognised the information, and to pique a curiosity in those younger spirits who had the stirrings of the search for meaning. Unfortunately both share also, the common characteristic that the information is not always explicit. But then much of spirit communication requires work to extract the gold from the prospector's pan of enquiry!

For four centuries almost, before the world had spiritual messages in the mass media, the Western world had principally Shakespeare's plays for cryptic clues and subliminal messages about the spirit dimension, for those who had the ability to spot them. As an example, in appendix one, I discuss some of the spiritual references in his play *"The Tempest"*.

I have read there are over one thousand books written about Shakespeare. As a playwright, poet and author, he has by far the most books listed on the British Library catalogue search engine with 10,461 entries. His legacy is enormous. I cannot say of those books how many (if any) discuss his life from the perspective of life-plan and spirituality. He is the only Spiritual Master in the top ten list. Gandhi and Mother Teresa are examples of recent high profile masters.

Oliver Cromwell, 1599 – 1658

Again it is necessary to put the life into context of the plan for the planet and the particular country of incarnation. England, as I have said, was destined to rise in importance, to be the first nation to industrialise, the first to shrug off religion's suffocating influence, to be the founder of an Empire and to exert global reach.

Amongst all of this greater plan, was the English Civil War. It was not a happenstance event, although it may have seemed it. Had Charles I not been so stubborn, for example, but more accommodating, the entire war may have been either avoided, or been much less protracted. But it was a predestined event.

Wars are a feature of nursery worlds only. Higher evolved life has long forsaken violence as a means of settling differences. It is a learning process for young spirit, and so features on planets mostly used by beginner spirits. The English Civil War had several spiritual purposes. Being a civil war, whole families were sometimes torn apart over it, thereby supplying the prop to learn about tolerance and acceptance of difference in beliefs.

It had a less obvious purpose; part of a scheme for the reduction and closure of earth energies. This is a topic I will explore in a later book, but for the moment, I can say that whenever human trauma takes place on an energy site, the energy flow is disturbed, much like an individual may suffer life-long from the emotional scarring of an event, even though the physical damage has long since healed. Many civil war battles took place on or near energy sites.

Choice of Parents:

Born into a family of minor gentry, neither rich nor paupers, he was the only son of three to survive. He had attentive parents. The family name is interesting; it was a Thomas Cromwell who was instrumental in the dissolution of the monasteries. For one with a destiny to similarly strike at the core of the establishment, the name may have been an influence in choice of parents.

Main Plot:

Cromwell's main plot was to be the military leader in the Civil War; to take part in many bloody battles; to cause the dethronement of the monarchy and as a leader to lead many to their destiny. The spiritual tests for him included compassion and tolerance once victory was achieved.

Past Lives:

Richard Holmes described him as "a fine, self-taught soldier, who mastered tactics and logistics and understood what makes men fight". I would add that he acquired these skills through past lives. He had no military training or experience prior to 1642, but from the beginning showed genius, and by 1646 was recognised as the best soldier in the land.

His Third:

In 1620, he married Elizabeth Bourchier, daughter of a City merchant, which was a happy union. Through her father, Cromwell makes contact with London merchants and leading Puritans. Her father was in fact his third.

Life-plan Coordination:

John Knox, a learned scholar, wrote *"The Reformation of Scotland"* outlining the process without which the British model of government under Oliver Cromwell would not have been possible.

Early Crossroads:

Whilst at Cambridge University, he leaves prematurely on his father's death in 1617. His academic career is cut short.

Subplot:

He suffered what might be described as a mental breakdown and underwent a conversion experience to the Puritan cause. His subsequent zeal for God gave him the inner strength for his later role. It also fixes him firmly in the anti-royalist camp (Charles I had long persecuted the Puritans). Religion fortifies his soldiers who marched into battle singing hymns.

Inner Knowledge:

1. After his conversion experience, he was seized by a sense of divine destiny. He said he felt as though he was waiting for God to give him a mission.

2. At the outbreak of civil war in 1642, he raised a troop of horse soldiers and took part in one of the earliest military actions (seizing the silver plate at Cambridge). Unbeknown to him, his role of cavalry leader would later be crucial in Parliament's victories.

3. Whilst Parliament advocated a negotiated settlement with the king, Cromwell wanted a total victory over the Cavaliers.

Subplot Failures:

1. He opposed the Leveller demands for universal suffrage and other social reforms (he shot some of their leaders). This holds back democracy for two centuries, until the Reform Act of 1832.

2. After a Royalist insurrection, Cromwell imposes a direct military dictatorship by dividing the country into districts, each with a major-general. This enhanced security, but was intensely unpopular. It lasted less than two years, but helped the cause for restoration – at least the King had not imposed military rule!

Numbers:

The number three and its multiple nine, sometimes have a spiritual significance in the plan for the planet and for individual life-plans, which is shown in Cromwell's life. September, the ninth month, is often chosen as the start or end of events (9/11 is a recent example, the World Trade Centre tragedy). Two of Cromwell's most decisive victories (Dunbar and Worcester) both took place on 3rd September. He also died on that day. The Second World War, too, began on that day. Certain numbers that can be seen in events are a clue to their planned nature. For example, the number of scud missiles the Iraqis fired in the 1991 Gulf War was thirty-nine. The numbers killed in the Zeppelin *"Hindenburg"* airship disaster at New Jersey in 1937 are reported variously between thirty-three and thirty-nine.

Spirituality:

His servant wrote, *"A larger soul hath seldom dwelt in a house of clay"*. It is easy to confuse his role with his spirituality; a great role, but not an old spirit. Like Churchill, he was a high level two spirit. (He has reincarnated subsequently a number of times and is currently level three).

John Lennon, 1940 – 1980

Choice of Parents:

His was not an easy start, as usual for a high-level spirit, chosen for the challenge and potential for spiritual growth. He had working class parents, his father left when he was an infant, followed by his mother two years later killed in a car accident when he was seventeen. He was then raised by an aunt. These circumstances provided two purposes; the lesson that one's parents are only one's parents biologically and secondly, the experiences provided a resource for some of his song-writing.

Subplot and re-script:

It was in his plan to suffer the loss of someone close to him. His mother did fulfil her part in this, but they were not as close as they might have been, although they were closer in his teenage years. An experience partially achieved, the guide scripted in that John met fellow student Stuart Sutcliffe at art college, who joins John's group on bass guitar. He dies prematurely in 1961, an event which deeply affected John. (Readers of *"Why Come Back?"* may recall this happened to me also, a rescripting of my mother's serious illness in my case).

Synchronicity Examples:

1. The group, having gained a local following in Liverpool, had an encounter with a local record shop owner turned manager, Brian Epstein. He became their manager, a necessary ingredient for their success, who helped them create their first number one.

2. Following a period of five years without writing a note, he had a brush with death while sailing in a storm to Bermuda. This is followed by a sudden creative fit in 1980. (He had forgotten his lines and needed a prompt).

3. His biographer Ray Coleman lists a whole catalogue of instances where the number nine features in Lennon's life. This detail would not be in the life-plan but would be scripted by his guide. Lennon recognised the recurrence of the number in his life. What his guide intended was for him to go on from that and realise that there was more at work in his life than mere chance.
    To give some of the instances, he was born on 9th October, so was his son Sean. Brian Epstein first saw the Beatles on 9th November 1961 and secured their record contract with EMI on 9th May. John met Yoko on 9th November. I comment further in Appendix Two on this number synchronicity.

Contingency Example:

Having been turned down by Decca, EMI gives the fledgling group a recording contract.

Past Life Connection Example:

He meets Cynthia Powell at art school. They marry in 1962. They had been partners in previous lives and their meeting and marriage in this one was in their life-plans.

His Third:

In 1966, John met Yoko Ono and almost immediately was drawn to her. He later acknowledged her as his mentor in life and artistic expression.

Crossroads Example:

John is married with a son. He finally leaves Cynthia for the avant-garde artist Yoko. They marry in 1969 and some of his best work is produced in 1970 and 1971.

Main Plot:

To make a unique contribution to popular music; often using himself as his own creative material born out of his experiences. He planned to use his music to further the cause of world peace.

When planning his life, he knew how Gandhi and Martin Luther King would use assassination to further their message of non-violence, and similarly chose such an end. He said he never understood why these great examples of non-violent people had died violently. Many events present a challenging spiritual paradox. What seems a cruel twist of fate, I describe as life-plan. Had they died peacefully, would we remember them and their message as well as we do?

Past Lives:

His actions in a military life previously had caused him to be sickened by violence and this unconscious memory drove him in his "peace" mission.

Human Weaknesses:

1. Forgivably, the huge popularity the Beatles enjoyed went to his head. His infamous comment, "We're more popular than Jesus now" damaged their reputation. The subsequent death threats hastened the break up of the band.

2. As John Cooper writes, "his carapace of truculent toughness" helps him through a difficult adolescence, but he is slow to remove the shell in later life when it is inappropriate.

3. His peace message is a one liner he fails to develop. He may have felt it did not need intellectual and moral elaboration, but if he had emphasised more that, "Humanity is all one," for example, this would have been simple, radical, provocative and morally supportive. Peace campaigners (e.g. anti-war with Iraq in 2003) have yet to use this rallying statement.

Spirituality:

Some "designer" elements can be seen in his life-plan. As a level four spirit one largely writes one's own life-plan within the constraints of the syllabus and the plan for the place of incarnation. His was an ambitious life-plan; his call for peace did rally many, but sadly not those in positions of influence.

His peace stand, whilst most laudable, was made in the safe environment of studios, shop windows or hotel bedrooms. One may contrast this with Gandhi's non-violence activities in India; his marches, his refusal to pay the salt tax and so on. These forced those in authority to take notice. Contrast also, the former American marine, who in January 2003, declared his intention to encourage as many Europeans as possible to go to Iraq in protest against the planned war, to make the authorities think before bombing their own people. The one a hands-on, "put myself at risk" course of action, the other, a statement only, although one made dramatically.

Gandhi, I am told, was a spiritual master and the marine I suspect is a level five spirit. One can see here the maxim, the older the spirit the more difficult the life-plan. The pop group, the "Beatles" were a varied mix in spiritual ages. They demonstrate that spiritual age has no relevance during the incarnation for human interaction of itself, but is relevant, of course, in complexity and degree of difficulty of the life-plan. All four would have been from the same soul group, i.e. they had already had at least one previous shared incarnation together, an illustration of the frequent preference of choosing familiar rather than unfamiliar spirit for major roles.

Diana, Princess of Wales, 1961 – 1997

Like my brother, she died tragically when aged thirty-six. The spiritual number three again making significant appearance.

Choice of Parents:

With her destiny to marry into the Royal family, a major aristocratic pedigree determined the choice. As neighbours at Sandringham, her family were to socialise with the Queen's family. Her parent's separation when she was aged six proved a challenge; she had a difficult relationship with her natural mother all her life. Her own family's break-up enabled her to identify more easily with misery forced upon others.

Main Plot:

To bring into question the deference for the Royal family, and in doing so, to bring into prominence the way we disempower ourselves in favour of all authority figures. Secondly, to show true popularity is earned, not by reason of position, but of deeds. Thirdly, to show through her funeral how, even if only momentarily, a world can be united across race, colour and creed.

Subplot Examples:

1. To experience bulimia; it was a means by which Charles could have drawn close to her if he had chosen to, by offering his support. Secondly, it earned her a good deal of sympathy later when it became public knowledge.

2. Her work for charities may have started out as a Royal duty, but through it and her success she was providing a lesson for all, on how to live life.

3. Her great affection for her two sons was an exercise in mother love. In contrast, the lack of affection from her husband will have taught her much about what love is not, in a marriage.

Human Weaknesses:

1. After the divorce and removal of her "HRH" title, her resignation from most of her charity and other patronages was a human reaction at the great slight she felt.

2. Her many love affairs were a cry for the affection which she had never had and an expression of the hurt Charles' long-standing adultery had caused.

Her Third:

This was Dodie Fayed; their relationship was quite brief, but the meeting momentous as without it she would not have been in Paris for the fatal car accident. An instance here, of thirds meeting late in an incarnation. The relationship took on an immediate intensity that would be surprising but for the fact that they had a spiritual connection.

Her Looks:

These were deliberately chosen for her role, as without them, achieving her main plot might not have been possible.

Synchronicity Examples:

1. The death of one of the Royal party in a skiing accident in March 1988 proves a pivotal experience. She finds the inner strength to control herself and to be her own person in coming forward to cope with tragedy and its consequences. For perhaps the first time she felt in command.

2. In her own words, *"All Sorts of people have come into my life – elderly people, spiritual people, acupuncturists, all these people came in after I finished my bulimia".* An illustration of the guide's role in getting actors to appear on cue.

Inner Knowledge:

1. She had a *"profound sense of destiny, a belief that she would never become Queen, as well as her awareness that she had been singled out for a special role,"* so wrote Andrew Morton, her biographer.

2. She said to her father when aged thirteen, *"I know I am going to marry someone in the public eye".*

3. In 1991 she said to Andrew Morton, *"I think I'm going to cut a very different path from everyone else. I'm going to break away from this set-up and go and help the man on the street".* She may have had advice from psychic people, who brought out or confirmed an inner recognition of her life-plan.

Past Lives Influence:

1. Skill – Not an academic by any means, but adept at manipulating and communicating through images. She had learned this skill elsewhere.

2. Choice of hobby – Her talent as a dancer as a girl suggests a past life influence. In 1976 she had won her school's

dancing competition. She maintained links with the English National Ballet even after she withdrew from other commitments.

3. Déjà vu – *"I've got a lot of that. Places I think I've been before, people I've met,"* she said.

4. "Care of people feelings" – As a teenager she undertook hospital voluntary visits and discovered she had a natural aptitude in forming an instinctive rapport with many patients. This points to her having had a nursing role in previous lives, or at least, roles in caring professions.

Spirituality:

The spirit that was Diana, belongs to a group of spirits that work for the welfare of the race of the place of incarnation. Hence her life-plan was not the norm for one of her spiritual age, which is comparatively young at level three. Her plan had the "approval" of other older spirit before her incarnation.

She had a great personal inward challenge in overcoming an unhappy marriage, low self-esteem and ill-health to transform herself into an almost saint-like figure. Her outer challenge showed its triumph in all the tributes following her death. The decline in the monarchy's popularity owes no little explanation to the part she played. The unprecedented emotional outpouring at her death, whilst incomprehensible to some, has left a lasting impression of how it is possible to unite all, irrespective of class, wealth, nationality and religion, even if only for one day.

Chapter conclusion:

My intention was not to "debunk" the famous. My apologies to the readers who have an admiration for one or more of the lives I have discussed. To use the mantra of The British School of Spiritual Knowledge, which I have co-founded, *"a change of perspective alters everything!"* I use the lives of the famous as they will have some familiarity to many people. All our lives will have a completely different appearance when seen through spiritual lenses. My purpose has been to show the most admired lives are roles certain spirit has chosen to play, and that the spiritual age of our heroes and heroines is not the same as their popularity ranking.

The life-plans described, in practice were far more complex, but I hope to have given a flavour or indication of them. Just as we wear many different suits of clothing through a lifetime, so each lifetime is but one suit the soul wears in its journey from a wardrobe provided by the Collective. My feeling is each spirit has a turn at a "famous life"; and the fact that one may be famous once, does not mean that one will be so again. Because I have used lives of the famous, the perception of what is the norm for a main plot may be distorted by these examples. The same lessons can be taught in much lower profile situations too.

With these examples of ten famous lives, one can now hopefully see the invisible made visible. The frustrated teenager who asks, "Why on Earth did I end up with you for parents?" may now see that there could be a life-plan reason. The choice of parents can be for the challenge of them (John Lennon, Winston Churchill and Isaac Newton, for example); can be essential for the main plot (Elizabeth I and Diana, for example); can be for the correct nurturing environment for the main plot (Isambard Kingdom Brunel and Charles Darwin, for example); or can be for a combination of these and for many other reasons too. In my own case, my mother was an older spirit and my father a younger one. I experienced a strong maternal bond but had (deliberately) a challenging father. The latter was a subplot in my life and neither parent had a bearing on my main plot, which is to write and teach.

One can see how society and our culture evolve through the influence of individual life-plans, which are pre-planned roles, which certain spirit chose to fulfil. The lives of Darwin, John Lennon and Diana were intended to impact upon popular thought; the lives of Newton, Darwin and Brunel to create technological and scientific advancement. Our war heroes of Cromwell, Churchill and Nelson, were just that, "war hero", but not great spirits. That description is reserved for Shakespeare, who held a mirror for us to discover ourselves. All the lives described will be merely one small episode in the total life of the spirits concerned. Most likely some of these spirits will have reincarnated and have now added other experiences to their portfolio.

The crossroads examples amongst the lives of the ten famous Britons show how a life-plan could have taken a radically different direction if a spiritually incorrect decision had been taken, but contingency planning would be in place so a plan may not have been permanently derailed.

Perhaps one of the most historically well-known contingency plans (but not as such) is the six wives of Henry VIII. He was destined to break from Rome so if either he or the Pope had acceded to one remarriage, others were in the plan to give a second and subsequent opportunity. This was such an important move that several contingencies were written into the plan. He did not have to take the choice to "change wife" each time after the first one had worked, but he did.

Having devoted my first chapter to spirit thirds, I trust the varied roles thirds can play is well illustrated. Quite often it is as life partner, as in the case of Churchill and John Lennon, but lover also as for Nelson and Elizabeth I. It may be a life-long friend such as it was for Darwin or a parent as in the case of Brunel. Sometimes the interaction is relatively brief but will always be momentous as illustrated by Newton, Shakespeare, Cromwell and Diana.

I have listed the "human faults" partly as a confirmation of the spiritual level, there being a rough inverse correlation between the two. Isaac Newton shows, for example, that we can be far from perfect even as a high level five spirit. The spirits who were Shakespeare and Darwin were the oldest in the ten examples. Not everyone becomes a Spirit Council member; only a small number do, but everyone becomes a spiritual master eventually.

I wrote at the beginning of my first book, that all of life is orchestrated and choreographed from spirit. That understandably would have many reactions of disbelief brought up as we are in a rational-scientific western culture. I trust the examples of crossroads, inner guidance, synchronicity and inner knowledge that I have given in this chapter, do now substantiate my previous statement, or at least, make the concept of life-plans and role of the guides easier to visualise.

The past lives explanation I have specified in my famous lives examples, would only be a part of their total influence. There is a myriad of ways our past lives influence the current one for each of us, and I devote a separate chapter now, to that theme.

CHAPTER FOUR

OUR PAST LIVES AND PRESENT CHARACTERS

The spiritual journey for all consists of hundreds of lives, both on planet Earth and elsewhere. I am told it is a feature of earthly incarnations alone, that we have temporary amnesia about our past lives when we arrive here, but full memory is restored once back in our natural spiritual state.

The reason we suffer this amnesia is so that our decisions are not affected by knowledge of our past lives. The Romans recognised that even a belief in reincarnation was not helpful for control purposes. They therefore removed all reference to the topic from the early Christian Bible when they adopted Christianity themselves. The test of our spirituality would not be the challenge it is here, if we brought all our knowledge with us.

However, to some extent, the amnesia is not complete in all cases, and we can access our past life memories. These fall into two categories, intentional memories and unintentional ones. Déjà vu is quite a common experience and can be both intentional and unintentional. Déjà vu is usually a memory of a past life triggered by something in the current one. The most common one is that of being in a place for the first time and it suddenly appearing familiar. The memory of being in the same place in a previous life is being accessed. Other triggers can include film clips, a brief track of music and so on. Sometimes past life memories are accessed during spiritual healing, and of course they can be in meditations, which is probably the most frequent instance.

Intentional memories are the deliberate inclusion in a life-plan of a particular memory. This can often be to set someone off on an investigation into past lives or at least a meaning to life. Sometimes when the past life memory results in a medical condition that defies conventional and even alternative therapy, a search into past lives can be for many, a last (but intended) resort. A guide may allow past life memories to appear during a regression experience to further encourage the incarnated counterpart on their spiritual journey, to provide a degree of "proof" that the spirit is indeed eternal.

My own past life regression experience is the single most important one that changed me from sceptic to eager pupil in the search to know more. This is not for everyone, only those who can accept the phenomenon (or who are judged by their guide to be accepting) will benefit from a regression experience. From recipient, I have now turned into a provider (quite unbelievably). I have now facilitated regression experiences for many others. Each one is a fascination in itself and the memories accessed are often given with a teaching purpose in mind too. The memories accessed are always controlled by the guides, so one cannot predict or specify in advance what will be seen.

Intentional memories can be for reasons other than spiritual awakening but still part of the life-plan. We have seen two character trait examples in the previous chapter, those of Horatio Nelson's lust for heroism and conversely, John Lennon's urge to give his peace message to the world, where unconscious past life memory was their driving force. We have encountered an example in mediumship of two people who have a mutual antagonism. The elder one spiritually, due to his advanced spiritual nature, could not hold any ill-feelings towards another. He deliberately chose in his life-plan to have the unconscious memory of previous lives shared with this other person, to provide himself with the challenge of understanding and forgiveness. The past lives were where one had treated the other badly. Those film scripts that have a character from a previous life play a tormenting role in a present life are not so far fetched!

Unintentional memories can be for one or more of the following reasons:

1. Sometimes a memory is not completely erased in the amnesia and becomes what we have termed a "fingerprint" memory. It usually appears inappropriately and often is the cause of fears and phobias. A painful or traumatic

experience in a past life may have been so etched in the memory that it has not been entirely wiped clean.

2. If the last incarnation was a recent one, which in spiritual terms is within the last one hundred years, and the death was violent and unexpected, then again the memory may not be totally erased. This is another regular explanation for fears and phobias. My own most recent past life fits this category, having been a First World War experience. It did not cause a phobia, but drew me always to stop and reflect at war memorials.

3. If the life is a repeat one quickly following a major life-plan failure, then its memory recall can be because of this familiar scenario.

4. Similarly, if use is being made of a similar set of circumstances because having worked well once, it was decided to use them again, then yet again a previous life memory can be unintentionally triggered.

5. As with déjà vu, a current life that has familiarity from repeat location, repeat scenario or use of familiar "supporting actors", can sometimes cause memories to be unintentionally experienced.

Past life therapy that involves a regression experience may often be successful in removing an unintentional memory that is causing problems and inappropriate emotions in the current life. If the guide sees that the memory is hampering the current life-plan from proceeding as intended, he may well engineer his incarnated counterpart to seek such therapy.

Angela, my partner, has had many enquirers for her past life mediumship. This is a question and answer mediumship process to access past lives without need of a regression. The enquirer merely asks if there is a past life explanation for something being currently experienced, and if so and their guide judges it correct, receives an explanation from spirit. Even though no recall of the incident is intentionally made, a description of the event or circumstances surrounding the emotional issue in the current life, has often prompted the actual memory, and so the therapeutic effect is achieved just as in regression.

Often Angela sees the memory herself in such circumstances and can describe it. To give one of many examples, one enquirer with a debilitating fear of stairs, commented that for her entire life, she had been badgered by her family about her "unreasonable fear". Having received details of severe injury sustained from a fall down a staircase in a previous life, she immediately felt better about herself because now she knew that the fear was not "unreasonable". Elevating it to the status of a "reasonable fear" had immediately diminished its thrall over her.

For the rest of this chapter, I have put together extracts from our mediumship casebook to show the many and varied ways our past lives have influenced or contributed to our present life characters.

In alphabetical order, the headings I have used are:

- ❖ Animals – liking for animals
- ❖ Children – "care feeling" towards children
- ❖ Compulsion
- ❖ Déjà Vu experiences
- ❖ Dislikes – various
- ❖ Dreams – explanation for vivid or recurring dreams
- ❖ Family Issues
- ❖ Fears and Phobias
- ❖ Feelings – strong or particular feelings
- ❖ Health Issues
- ❖ Likes, Attractions and Interests
- ❖ Occupation and Talent
- ❖ Places – a draw to or liking of a particular place
- ❖ Relationship Issues

Here are the actual case summaries with the names omitted or changed, to preserve confidentiality:

Animals

1. **Past Life Connection with Animals** – A lady asked if she had past lives connected with animals. Her guide answered that her love of animals has manifested itself in

many lives. She had a life in which she was an "elephant boy" in India. This was a life in which a sense akin to telepathy exists between boy and beast.

2. The same lady also had a life in which she was the daughter of a wealthy merchant in Florence, and surrounded herself with animals, being indulged in this by her father who shared her love of them.

3. **Bond with Animals** – A male enquirer had a strong bond with animals. He felt he experienced something akin to telepathy with them and they seem drawn to him. His guide confirmed that he had lived more than one incarnation in which animals have featured strongly. One of the strongest connections was in an aboriginal life in which he possessed the aboriginal ability to communicate thought to animals. He was never in danger from them due to this ability and they recognised him as a kindred spirit and as having an empathy with them. This was in Australia his life being 1204 to 1242. This was a skill that was passed down through the generations. He has retained something recognisable by animals through many subsequent lives. He had three children in that life and each of the three inherited, or learned his gift.

4. **Dogs** – A lady really liked animals, dogs in particular. The answer to this was that this relates to a life in which she was the wife of a hunt master in the early 1800s. Her entire life was surrounded by dogs, and she was the one mainly called to help with the birth of the puppies. Her life would have felt as if it had a piece missing if she had not had a dog with her in the home.

Children

1. **Past Life Connection with Children** – A lady wished to know if she had done anything in her past lives connected with children. Her guide answered that she had a life in which she was a tutor, male in that incarnation. This was in France in the late 1600s. In an occupation usually

followed through necessity rather than calling, she was unusual in the degree of care she actually had for her charges and the empathy she had with the children that passed through her care.

2. In a life from 1519 to 1598, the same lady had a life in England in which she was a children's nurse. This was a life in which she never married, making her home in that of her employers, even after the children she had in her care had long grown. She would delight in their visits in which they brought their own children, who would be again in her care. Her name in that incarnation was Alice Beckham.

Compulsion

1. **Moving House** – A lady enquirer had moved house ten times within the last two years. The expense was becoming a problem, let alone the affect on her family. Her guide explained that she has to date, experienced many lives where permanency was not a feature. This has been for a variety of reasons. On a simple level, she has had five recent nomadic lives, lives as a Bedouin, an Eskimo and a Hungarian Gipsy among them. A feature of these lives was the need to move in order to survive. This has left her with a "fingerprint memory" in this incarnation, of needing to move for survival. This accounts for her becoming unsettled after too long in one place.

    She recently had an incarnation in the Second World War, in which she was part of the resistance in France, and again had to keep moving to avoid detection and to survive.

    In this life, there is no need for this. She has brought this feeling through inappropriately in the current incarnation, and this is why she feels so weary of it. At some level, she knows that she is not supposed to do this, but she cannot seem to help it. It is a deep survival instinct that is misplaced this time. Now that she knows the reason she will find that she is able to address the problem.

2. **Cleaning** – A lady enquired if her obsessive-compulsive disorder of constant cleaning and being a perfectionist had a past life connection.

    Her guide advised that she had a life in the 1300s in Germany, when she was the mother of six children. In that life she was not poor, but not nobility either. The Black Death was sweeping the country and she saw the hovels of the poor where the disease struck. In fear for her own children, she cleaned and cleaned in order to prevent, she thought, the disease of squalor overtaking them.

Déjà Vu

1. **Long Episodes of Déjà Vu** – An enquirer often experiences amazing feelings of déjà vu, which can last quite some time. Her guide explained by saying she has very nearly brought with her past life recall this time. It is not quite there, but her regular and prolonged experiences of déjà vu are only a few steps away from it. Should she seek past life regression or use meditation and self hypnosis techniques with the express purpose of exploring her many past lives, she would soon find that this developed into instantaneous recall, her guide felt.

2. **Déjà Vu when Watching a Film** – A male enquirer reported a strange feeling while watching the film *"Titanic"*. There was a scene after the ship had sunk, in which the girl was suffering from the cold, staring up at a star studded sky. As he watched this, he "remembered" lying on the cold ground, feeling the cold spreading throughout his body and looking at a sky just like it. Was this a past life memory as he had thought? His guide replied that he had, in a previous incarnation, worked in the court of Tsar Nicholas at the time of the 1917 revolution. He went with the family into exile in Siberia and when the mob came for them for execution, tried with another trusted aid to rescue the children. They managed to spirit away Anastasia but he was killed in the process, leaving his partner, who is his father in this life, to carry on alone. The feeling he had experienced when watching the

film was triggered because he had indeed laid on the ground, looking at the sky as his life blood ran away. His name in that life was Alovsha Danylko. He was born in 1880 and died on that fateful day of 16 July 1918. The enquirer, although British in the current life, has occasionally been mistaken for a Russian, and now understands why.

3. **Déjà Vu Triggered by Music in a Video Game** – A lady enquirer believed she experienced a flash of a past life which was set off by a music clip. The guide explained that what she sees, is a life in France at the time just before the 1789 revolution. She was an aristocrat, the daughter of a nobleman and the room that she feels is a room high up in a chateau. The windows are open and music is playing as she prepares for her wedding. The people in the avenue that she is aware of in the flashback are waiting to cheer her carriage.

Dislikes

1. **Dislike of Churches** – An enquirer did not like churches. He wished to know if there was a reason for this aversion. His guide explained that he was a Teutonic Knight, which was a German military and religious order of knights and priests, who broke away from the Catholic church to become Lutherans. Following this, he was murdered by a Catholic agent of the Pope in the entrance to a church in 1527. The agent had a mission to kill the leader of the order and was surprised by the enquirer who was not really the intended target. His third in this life was a fellow knight.

2. **Dislike of Orientals** – A lady enquirer felt embarrassed, but had a strong dislike of Orientals. She harboured no prejudices relating to race normally, but just did not feel any affinity with Chinese, Japanese or Koreans. Her guide was able to shed light on it for her. In 1639 Japan was closed to Europeans. At this time, the lady was a trader in the area, an Italian named Henricus Marzarius, employed

in the pursuit of bringing oriental artefacts to the West. When the Europeans were "evicted", they were supposed to leave behind all acquisitions. Hernricus tried to leave with his spoils but was caught and imprisoned for it for some time. He was released and returned to Italy to his family but always had a dislike for Orientals following this experience. He went on to become a wealthy merchant and died in 1679. Could she know where he lived, she enquired? The guide confirmed that he lived in Monteperti.

3. **Dislike and Suspicion of Arabs** – A male enquirer had similar feelings to the lady above, but this time about Arabs. He had worked in Arab countries for much of his working life and been invited to the homes of the locals as a friend, but he could not rid himself of a feeling of distrust around them. His guide advised him that this was not really surprising. In a past life from 1220-55, he was Abdal Sami, an Arab living on the coast of Kenya, during the building of the great palace and main mosque at Gedi. He was in charge of some of the design and in particular the zullah and mihrab, the prayer hall and the niche. The materials used in here were Yemenites blacks and yellow, and mustard wares. They had a plaster floor in the niche. He met with an accident in the building, was crushed by a fall of materials and perished. The accident was not really an accident at all, it was arranged by one who coveted his position and who he had felt distrust of for a long time. Another detail was that his daughter of that life is actually his wife in the current incarnation.

Dreams and Meditation Issues

1. **Dream of Rescuing Paintings from a Burning Building** – An enquirer has a recurring dream about rescuing paintings from a burning building. His guide explained that it originated from his life in the English Civil War period. This life as a Parliamentarian, was quite an eventful life for him. Prior to the outbreak of the hostilities, there was a fire in the home of the master for whom he worked. He and others were called upon to

rescue the paintings from the great hall at severe risk to
their own lives. A great friend of the enquirer's perished in
the blaze and he nearly lost his own life too. The master,
however, was more concerned with the safety of his
precious paintings and did not show any remorse at the
loss of life. That was a contributing factor to the enquirer
joining the Parliamentarian forces.

2. **Temples and Pillars** – During meditation, a lady
enquirer often got images of temples and pillars (Greek
perhaps) and had an affinity with Atlantis. Her guide
advised that she had experienced many ancient lives. She
had lived lives in Ancient Greece, Rome, Egypt and
Atlantis too, so it would have been unusual if she did not
receive such images.

3. **Trees in Grey and White** – A lady enquirer had a
recurring dream in which she was battling her way
through trees, she was frightened, but didn't know why.
She saw the trees as grey and white and when she woke,
could "taste" the dream. Her guide laid her fears to rest by
confirming that this was a past life scenario, and in no way
related to the current incarnation. It related to a life in
which she lived in France. Following the Mistral in the
year 1202, there was a forest fire near the village. She and
her family were obliged to leave their home. She was
Abella Leger, six years old, and the dream of grey and
white trees relates to the ash and the smoke surrounding
the trees. The "taste" is the taste from the acrid smoke,
which lingered long after the fire. Although the danger
was imagined rather than real, the child was frightened
although not really sure why. This is why the feeling
stayed with her, the experiencing of fear without knowing
why. When the reason is understood, the mind can
assimilate the information and "file" it for future use.
When the reason is not understood, it is harder to file it
away.

4. **Riverboat Steamer** – A lady had a recurring dream
involving what appears to be a riverboat steamer, in which

she saw a friend from this life too. Her guide gave the past life explanation. This life was in the American South, and she was Aline Semple, born in Kentucky. She was with her friend Jenny and their husbands, Benicia and Robert, taking a trip to celebrate their wedding anniversaries, which were within days of each other. An explosion on board, caused the boat to sink, and while both ladies were rescued, both the men tragically were drowned.

She further enquired, why she would have this dream when she did, what was it trying to tell her? Her guide explained that in that life, Aline never remarried. She missed her life lesson by refusing to move on. There will be events in her current life which will open a path for her to move her life onwards and this was her guide's attempt to counsel her not to miss taking the opportunity when it presents itself, even though at first she may not feel as if she wants to take that route.

Family Issues

1. **Problem Relatives** – An enquirer had a problem in that she sensed her sister-in-law was jealous of her and her family, and suspected she grasped every opportunity to stir up trouble for them. This worried her greatly as she did not know what she had done to this woman to deserve such malice. Her guide advised that in a previous life, the relative in question was passed over by a man for whom she had affection, when he chose the enquirer instead. From the rest of that lifetime, she felt animosity for the enquirer, the man and their family. As so often happens, the spirits have incarnated into each other's lives again quite quickly and the relative feels resentment and jealousy towards the enquirer and her family in this current life, without even understanding herself why this is so. She just feels a need to cause trouble; she feels jealous but could not say herself what she is jealous of. The guide advised that there is no answer to this problem for the enquirer. It would require the relative in question to seek spiritual guidance and possibly have past life regression or mediumship in order for the matter to be resolved, which

was of course, most unlikely given the person's lack of acceptance of spirit.

2. The same enquirer felt that her nephew, the son of her sister-in-law, also harboured resentment towards the family. It transpired that in the life just detailed, he was actually his mother's brother. In that past life he had observed the slight to his sister, which because of the culture of the life, was a slight for the family. Although not affected as acutely by it, living within the sphere of his mother's animosity in this life has reawakened some of his own feelings, but to a lesser extent.

3. **Family Discord** – An enquirer had noticed that her adult daughter and the daughter's own daughter, the enquirer's granddaughter, seemed to be unable to avoid antagonising each other. They seemed to share a bond as mother and daughter, but could never be long in each other's company without the antagonism surfacing. The guide replied that they had shared a past life as sisters. The one who is now the mother in this life, was her father's favourite in the past life as she was the more attractive of the two, while the one who is now the daughter, was the more intelligent. They have brought through the feelings of rivalry into the current incarnation, and whilst the situation should improve as the child ages, they will never be fully understanding of each other.

Fears and Phobias

1. **Fear of Birds** – An enquirer wished for an explanation as to why she had this unreasonable fear. Her guide said this was related to her having a past life in the eighteenth century in India. She observed some carrion birds busily at work on a corpse that had suffered execution and the memory has left a very vague unease within her. She has worked through this to a degree in this current life. The lesson in the previous life was, however, not to fear the birds, but realise the real villain of the peace was man. The birds were only following their natural instinct.

2. Another enquirer with the same fear, discovered that she was a French soldier in the late 1400s. During a campaign, she was wounded and left for dead on the battlefield. She regained consciousness to find the carrion crows pecking at her body. This is a carried memory from that life. This was in 1453, when Bordeaux, occupied by the English, fell to the French.

3. **Fear of Driving** – This enquirer had a mental block about driving. She wished to know if she should force herself, as her inability to drive was the cause of much inconvenience in her life, or if she should follow her instincts to leave well alone. Her guide confirmed that she was correct to follow her instincts in this case and went on to explain that she has the block due to a past life in which she met her demise while the driver of a vehicle. This was in America in the late 1800s. In many cases, knowledge of the incident can remove the block, but in this case as the incident was quite horrific, it is ingrained in her in this, the next incarnation. It would be best to leave this as an area she does not venture into in this particular incarnation, she was advised.

4. **Fear of Fire** – An enquirer had a fear of fire until she reached the age of twenty, at which point it disappeared. Her guide told her of a life in which she and her child were trapped in a burning building. She was nineteen at the time and the child was only one year old. She could not reach her daughter and experienced terror, not for herself, but in her mother's torment for her child. This carried through as a fear of fire until she passed the age of the event in this life.

5. Another lady enquirer had a real fear of fire, to the point where at one stage she could not strike a match. Her guide explained this by saying she had experienced a life at the time of Queen Mary Tudor, the time known as the Bloody Terror. In that life she was a protestant, a young wife of a farmer. Her name in the incarnation was Kate Hornby.

She and her husband refused to convert to the Catholic faith and both went to the stake for their beliefs. This is where the fear of fire comes from. Kate was twenty-four years of age at the time, this was in 1556, and the enquirer's fear of fire will now diminish as she grows older, although she will always have a "healthy respect" for it her guide advised. (The enquirer confirmed that she had just this year turned twenty-four and indeed her fear is lessening.) Kate lived in Sussex in that life. Her husband's name was Harry.

6. **Fear of Snakes** – This enquirer, in common with many, had a real terror of snakes, to the point that she could not watch one on T.V., let alone observe a real one. If she were to turn a page in a book and find a picture of one overleaf, she would drop the book or fling it from her. Her guide told her of a life in which she was a young male who suffered a bite while on a hunting expedition. Because of the time and the culture she lived in, such a bite was always fatal and the death in this case was painful. This has manifested as a terror of the creature in this life.

7. **Fear of Small Spaces** – A common phobia this one. In the case of this enquirer, he had a life as a miner in Wales from 1742 to 1796. His name in this life was David Thomas. He died in a cave-in along with four others. They were too deep to be reached in time and died of suffocation. The fear of being trapped had carried through into this life. As the information was given to him, he had a flashback and relived the event. His fear has lessened since.

8. Another enquirer suffering the same fear found that it related to a life in China in the early 1100s. He was a monk in that life in a particular order that offended the emperor of the time. He and his fellows were walled up in the building of the monastery and left there to die. This was a regular fate for those whose religious beliefs offended the emperor, and explained the enquirer's attitude to religion in the current life, too.

9. **Fear of the Sound of a Knife Sharpening** – An enquirer had a real terror every time he heard this sound. His blood literally ran cold. Could he know if this had a past life connection, he wondered? His guide recounted a life in Spain in which he was a female living from 1692 to 1715 named Rosa Dansigeo. She was married against her will to a butcher, much older than she. Last thing every night he would sharpen his knives before retiring and this would signal to her his imminent arrival in the bedchamber, a thing she dreaded. Eventually he found her having a liaison with the young man she had hoped to marry, but who was not approved by her parents, and slit both their throats with one of his knives. The hatred of the sound comes from it being a signal of his retiring for the night rather than from the death, however.

10. **Fear of Stairs** – Another lady had a fear of stairs, especially stairs in old buildings and castles and of open tread stairs. Her guide explained that she had a life as a lady's maid in France, in the mid-1600s. In that life she was Adelisa. She suffered an accident while descending the stairs of the chateau where she worked. She had arms full of linen and the stairs were spiral, stone steps. She slipped on them and fell, suffering terrible injury as a result. She had to return home and live with her parents, no longer able to walk from her injuries. (This was a double explanation for the enquirer, as she is physically unable to walk unless she can see her feet, so cannot carry a tray or a basket of laundry!)

11. **Fear of Spirit and Ghosts** – A lady asked why she, although spiritual, has a fear of actually seeing spirit or a ghost. The answer related to a life in which she had great spiritual ability. Unfortunately, the time of the life was such that to have this ability was to be considered a witch. She tried to keep it under cover so that it was not known, but her spiritual nature gave her a sense of inner peace that set her apart and it was sensed by those in her immediate vicinity. She was persecuted for this and eventually executed as a witch. In this life since this time,

145

she has subconsciously associated spiritual contact with her brutal death. It is not the spirit itself that would bring fear to her, but in her mind, it is being in communication with spirit that is frightening.

12. **Fear of Heights** – A lady asked why she had this fear. This relates to a life in which she was experiencing a male incarnation in the 1500s and was engaged in the building of a church. She was working on carvings in the roof, when the scaffold she was on collapsed. She held on to a buttress, but fell before help could reach her. This is something that reappears in her lives occasionally since that time. The church in question was being built in York and the date of the fall was 14 August 1568.

Feelings

1. **"Care of People" Feelings** – A male enquirer had strong feelings that he should have "care of people", that he should be in a position in which he was entrusted with this, and a feeling that he had done this before somewhere. His guide was happy to confirm that among his past lives, he had lives as a teacher, a political figure and a senator. In all of these incarnations he had taken his responsibility seriously, looking to the good of the people he had in his care, rather than to his own advancement, as did so many with responsibilities such as this.

2. **Mistrust of Others** – An enquirer who we met earlier in this document, reported a strong mistrust of other people, so much so, that it had caused problems in his life as he was unable to fully open himself to others, including his wife and family. His guide confirmed that in some of his past lives, whenever he had left one "camp" and given his allegiance to another, which he had done on more than one occasion, it usually ended with problems for him, not least loss of his life. In the English Civil War, he had left his Royalist master to fight for the cause of the Parliamentarians and lost his life. In his life as a Tutonic Knight, he left the Catholics and aligned himself with the

Lutharians and lost his life. He had other lives in which
the end result was not as dramatic, but still unfavourable.
This is a recurring pattern in his lives, one of the grass
always being greener on a different side, and one that has
led to mistrust of others, but is only a product of the choices
he has made in his lives so far. If he were to trust others
more, this would be the first step to his soul being able to
settle down and start its progression.

3. **Something Missing** – An enquirer had a feeling like a
   void in her life, as if something was missing but she was
   unable to identify what it was. Her guide advised that she
   was fortunate to have had spiritual awareness in her last
   three incarnations, but due to the time of those
   incarnations had to practice this in a clandestine manner
   for fear of persecution. This has left a "fingerprint" on the
   current incarnation, a feeling of something missing from
   her natural routine; a little like an empty corner where
   something once stood and only a vague memory of what
   was there. She had planned for this incarnation to use her
   spiritual abilities more openly, but to do this when certain
   other chapters of her life were completed. Her guide
   advised her that now was the time, she could happily go
   forward and fill the void in her life.

4. **Lack of Self-motivation and Self-belief** – A lady
   enquirer asked if there was a past life explanation for her
   feeling this way. Her guide answered that this relates to a
   life in which she was experiencing a male incarnation. She
   was the eldest male son of an aristocratic family in France
   in the 1600s. She was constantly being verbally abused by
   her father of that life, a tyrannical man, who was actually
   jealous of his son, who had a greater intelligence than the
   father. The father felt invalidated by this and shored up
   his own esteem by destroying his son's. In several lives
   since this one, she has had a battle with esteem, and needs
   to work through the reason for it so it does not affect her
   incarnations in future. Meditation, regression or healing
   can assist with this. She needs help to "let go" the effects of
   the bullying father as they have no place in the current life.

5. **Self-esteem Problem** – A young enquirer wished to know if there was a past life explanation for his self-esteem problem. The guide answered that in his last life, he was the son of a bullying father. He was constantly being verbally berated and told he was useless and would never amount to anything. In that life he became withdrawn and insecure, he had no personal validation. In the current life, he has brought through a fingerprint from that past life, a vague memory that he is not conscious of, but that he needs to let go. It is not affecting him as deeply as it did last time, but even so it is having a drastic effect on his life and happiness. It was a lesson for that past incarnation and needs sending back there through meditation and visualisation.

    [As a footnote, this same enquirer asked if he had ever been a king in a past life as he had previously been told that he had. His guide confirmed that he was a king in Africa in a life in the 1300s. An example of how we must experience everything. As a king, I am sure his problems did not include a lack of self-esteem!]

6. **Feeling blocked** – A lady, whom I will call Meg, confessed that if ever she tries to do anything for herself she feels blocked. This is a past life situation from a life in the mid-eighteen hundreds in which she was a stepdaughter in the home of her father, a parish priest. She was much put upon by her father's second wife and when children were born to her, she treated Meg as a maid rather than a daughter.

    This is a real Cinderella story. Meg was so used to having to work for others, so often interrupted in any pursuit of her own, that she came to feel almost guilty at having any time to pursue her own interests in reading, needlework and painting. She has brought this through into this life, in that whenever she tries to do something for herself she stops herself, an inner feeling that it is wrong to follow her own interests which leads to this blockage when she tries. (Her pleasures in this life, were she able to follow them, would be reading, needlework and painting!)

Health Issues

1. **Arm Problems** – An enquirer had a problem with her
    right arm, which manifested as her relationship with her
    husband ended. She was curious as to the timing and
    wondered if her guide could shed any light on this. Her
    guide advised that this was a past life issue that has
    encroached into the current incarnation. The spirit that is
    now her ex-husband had been involved with her once before
    and the relationship that time had ended in a most abrupt
    manner, much as had the current one, but for different
    reasons. The life in question was in the mid-1700s when
    the enquirer was in a male incarnation as a member of a
    coalition of Afghan forces under Ahmad Shah Durrani. In
    1761, they were engaged in the defeat of the Maratha army
    at Panipat and her ex-husband was a fellow soldier. The
    two of them were holding a position and when the fighting
    reached its most dangerous, her ex-husband had
    abandoned his post and deserted. The enquirer had tried
    unsuccessfully to prevent him and within a few minutes of
    his departure had suffered injury to his arm, which later
    resulted in amputation. Without realising the connection,
    on the departure from her life of this spirit, she was
    affected by the past life memory. Her guide was confident
    the she would now let go the "unknown trouble" with her
    arm.

2. **Shoulder and Lower Back Pain** – An enquirer had right
    shoulder tendonitis and lower back pain. She had sought
    healing for these problems, but the pain still remained.
    She wondered if her guide could shed any light on this for
    her. She was advised that both of these conditions, and
    certain other aches and pains in the current incarnation
    had a past life connection for her. In a previous life she
    had suffered a fall, resulting in injuries so severe that she
    had suffered paraplegia. The current shoulder and lower
    back pain were where the injuries of that other life were
    the most severe. She was advised that her surgery and
    healing had corrected any physical problem and that the
    remaining pain required past life healing to be removed.

149

3. **Pain in the Jaw** – An enquirer has a problem with her jaw. Although diagnosed, none of the conventional, or indeed alternative, treatments have helped her. Her guide answered that the explanation lies in her last incarnation, which is why the memory of it is so strong in her. In that life she was Milly Tavner, an American, living in Chicago. She was involved in a motor accident and suffered a broken jaw as a result. This was in 1945. She suffered pain from it for years following and has "remembered" the pain into this life. She will find relief through regression therapy or by various alternative therapies, but conventional treatments will not address the past life influence.

4. **Female Health Problems** – This lady had lots of what we term women's health problems and could not get a diagnosis for them. Her guide explained the past life origin. In her last three lives she has had issues with this and it all stems from a life in which they caused her great difficulty. The life in question was in the early 1500s. She was the wife of a man involved in government of the country in which they lived and suffered a tragic stillbirth, which left her with difficulties thereafter. Because of these difficulties she was unable to bear children, something that caused problems for her for the rest of her marriage, as at the time, production of a son and heir was considered the duty of every wife. Since then, in three of her lives, the memory of the unhappiness of that incarnation has resulted in production of these gynaecological problems for her.

    We first saw this lady in November 2002. At that time her guide advised her to use alternative medicine, regression and visualisation to rid herself of the problem. She used visualisation alone and when we saw her again in March 2003 the problem had disappeared. She had a conventional examination previously arranged and by the time it came around they found no problem except some inexplicable scarring! We are pleased to report this success.

Likes, Attractions and Interests

1. **Attraction to the Military** – A male enquirer had strong
   feelings about the military. In this lifetime he had been
   desperate to join and wondered if there was a previous
   connection to account for this obsession. His guide advised
   that he had many military incarnations; it was a choice he
   often made when writing his life-plan. There were many,
   but a notable one was as Robert Guiscard, a Norman, who
   took Bari in Southern Italy in 1065, ending five centuries of
   Byzantine rule.

2. **Attraction to People in History** – We had an enquirer
   who wished to know if she had ever met Mary Queen of
   Scots. She felt an attraction so strong, it was as if she
   really knew her. Her guide advised that the reason she
   had such a strong affinity was that she was involved in the
   care of Mary, when she was a child at the French court.
   She cared for and loved the child to such a degree that it
   was almost a mother love. When she heard of Mary's
   death, she felt a void within her for the rest of her life.

3. **Historic Figures** – Another enquirer was inexplicably
   attracted to Richard III. So strong was her attraction, that
   it was almost an obsession. She had books about him on
   her shelves, pictures of him on her walls and belonged to a
   "Richard III" society. Her guide gave her the following past
   life details, which shed light on her attraction for her. In
   the past life in question she was Katherine Neville, a
   cousin of Richard. Her father was Edward, Baron
   Abergaven, the brother of Richard's mother, and her
   mother was Cicely Neville. She had many questions on
   this life, addressed over a period of time to her guide,
   including details of her demise, her husband and his name
   and her son. Even though such a "fan", neither she nor her
   friend from the "society", had heard of Katherine, and the
   details regarding her father Edward were few and far
   between. Eventually, however, they were able to track
   down a sketchy reference to her, which was enough to
   verify most of the details. Not really a "famous" life as it

was so difficult to find, but certainly one documented in history.

4. The above life piqued the curiosity of the friend mentioned above. Although not quite as obsessed as the original enquirer, she was almost as much obsessed with the Neville family, not just Richard III. Her guide related details for her of her life as Isabella Neville. This was actually a person who the enquirer had always viewed as being rather a "weak and silly" woman. In this current incarnation, the enquirer is a woman of iron will and fierce temper. It was easy to see the experiencing of different sides of a coin in comparing the two incarnations. Details given did however shed a new light on Isabella for the enquirer, who could see with more compassion why she was the way she appears from recorded details.

5. **Flowers, Aromatic Oils and Similar** – A lady enquirer had a strong liking for flowers, aromatic oils and the like. They had a big effect on her and if her home was not strongly perfumed it felt unnatural to her. This was a cause of some irritation to her husband as she constantly burned incense, aromatic oil or joss sticks, and he was not keen on the fragrance, saying he could "taste" it. She had long felt there was a reason behind this that was at the very edges of her memory, but just beyond recall. Her guide gave the following explanation.

   The reason for this related to an ancient life and it was an indication of her inner spirituality that she had accessed it in the way she had, almost reaching her own answer for it. The life was in Greece approximately 650BC. She was the wife of a merchant who dealt in the supply of fragrance to the nobility. She lived in a home surrounded by the various scents and would visit the building in which workers produced the oil from flowers, herbs and other botanicals. She had retained some of the memory this time, and this was why her home did not feel right in this life unless it was fragranced.

6. **Liking of Music** – An enquirer wished to know if she had ever been musical. She had a passion for music in this life and her greatest regret was being unable to play an instrument. Her guide told her that music and all things artistic had played a strong role in many of her life-plans previously. In particular, in her last incarnation she had a gift for the piano. Music was a "prop" she frequently chose to complement her life-plans.

7. **Drums** – A young male enquirer had a strong draw to drums. Not just the type used by pop and rock groups, but native drums, bongos, orchestral drums and so on. His "dream" was to make his living playing the drums. This was more than the usual teenage boy's dream of being a pop star. His guide confirmed that he had experienced several lives in which drums had been significant, including native lives. In the incarnation prior to the current one, however, he had been a part-time drummer. He worked as a mechanic during the day, but was part of a band that played for dances and events locally. While not famous, they were well known in their own area. Having brought back the "drumming" memory, it was therefore no coincidence that in this current incarnation, he is considering a career as an engineer or mechanic.

8. **Harpsichord** – A male enquirer had a love of harpsichord music, and found this rather strange, so wondered if we could clarify this, please?
    His guide gave details of a past life in which he was Francois Couperin, born in 1668. Francois was a composer of harpsichord music. He composed sacred and secular vocal music, organ music, motets and instrumental chamber music. He died in 1773.

9. **Interest in the English Civil War** – A male enquirer reported feeling drawn to the period of the English Civil War in 1642. Nothing definite, just an interest in it and he wondered if this indicated a spiritual connection, please? His guide gave details of a life as a farm labourer in this period on the estate of a Royalist, but joined the fight on

the side of the Parliamentarians. He was killed at Edgehill early in the fighting, aged 32. In this life he was Francis Wainwright. He was married, his wife being called Ann, and had four children, Kate, Ann, Francis and Samuel. This life was shared with the same third as the current life, who was his son Francis in that incarnation.

10. **Attraction for Castles** – A male enquirer had an attraction for castles and the coastline, and if they come together, so much the better. Could he know why this was? His guide responded that he had lived a life in which castles would have played a part. He was Edward Neville, Baron Abergavenny, born in 1412 and died 1467. In the current life the lady in number three and this gentlemen are very close friends.

11. **Interest in Earth Energies** – A male enquirer wondered if he had any past life connection with earth energies as he had a very strong interest in them in the current life. His guide confirmed that he was a worker with earth energies in a life from 1244 to 1204BC. He lived near the site on which Glastonbury now stands and was trained by a very knowledgeable earth healer at the time. His interest in this life is no accident and he will be closely involved with this in the future, should he so wish.

12. **A Love of Stars** – A lady enquirer was drawn to the stars and spent literally hours just gazing at them. Her guide gave past life reasons for this. She had a male incarnation in Spain in which she was engaged in the teaching of seamen to navigate by the stars. This occupied her entire life and instilled in her a fascination for them.

    She also had a life in Tudor England, where as a young woman of high birth she spent many hours without activities, and used observation of the stars to fill her time. This was not scientific observation but more of the dream study variety.

13. **A Fascination with Water** – A lady enquirer had puzzled why this was so. Her guide advised that water has played

a part in many of her lives. Her male incarnations have
included three seafaring ones. She has lived near the sea
many times and has one life in which the sea was the
means of her demise. Fortunately, there was little trauma
with this, it happening quickly, so it has not given her any
phobia. The lives near the sea were in Ireland, Africa and
Finland. The lives as a sailor were in Spain, Africa and
England.

Occupation and Talent

1. **Craftsman** – A lady enquirer wondered if she had a past
    life involvement as a craftsman. She felt strongly
    emotional when viewing an exhibition of this nature in
    something like a rural life museum. Her guide answered
    that this was most intuitive of her. She had a life in
    England in the 1800s when she lived in Devon. She was a
    blacksmith, male of course in that incarnation.

2. **Healer** – An enquirer who is a Reiki Master in the current
    incarnation wished to know if she had lives connected with
    healing previously, as her course this time always had a
    feeling of familiarity to it. Her guide answered that she
    had a series of lives relating to the care of others, both on a
    physical and mental level. Her chosen lives have reflected
    care of emotional health and well being and care of the
    physical, and this has led her to work through her own
    journey quite successfully. Although there were several
    lives in which this featured, he did relay details of some of
    the more major ones as a healer in India in the early 1700s,
    a healer in China in the early 1400s and a life as a doctor
    in the late 1600s when she had followed an interest in what
    we would now term "mental health" in a clandestine
    fashion, and a life in Kent in the mid-1500s when she was
    the equivalent of a midwife in her community and the one
    who everyone sought when there was a death or when
    nursing was required.

3. A lady asked if she had any connection with healing. Her
    guide confirmed that healing and teaching is a theme that

had permeated her lives on many occasions. She had been a doctor in Germany, a midwife in England and a mystic healer in a life in America, in which she was considered a witch.

4. **Nurse** – Another enquirer was advised of lives in the caring professions including that of doctor on more than one occasion. In this life, she has within her life-plan to become a spiritual surgeon, should she so choose. She is currently a healer, but had an inner feeling that this was not the goal she was supposed to strive for.

5. **Teacher** – An enquirer, a teacher in this life, felt so "at home" with her occupation, she wondered if she had been a teacher previously. It was all she ever wanted to do in life this time. Her guide confirmed that she had indeed been a teacher in past lives. In the life prior to the current one she had been a governess and, on hearing this, she could see herself in the life. She had also had four other lives as a teacher or scholar.

6. **The Stage** – A lady enquirer had a feeling that she has been on the stage in some form or other, can we clarify this please? Her guide detailed two incarnations in which entertaining has played a part. She was a female travelling player in Hungary in the 1760s. She lived a full and varied life, never having much in a material sense, but finding fulfilment and joy in her life. She never felt the lack of material possessions, she had little need for them, finding all she required in her life style. The other incarnation was as a performer in 1870 on the stage in London's West End. She was a singer, not a famous one but popular with the audience. She specialised in "character" songs.

7. **Presence and Charisma** – A male enquirer reported that he is found to be familiar to several people in any gathering. Why is it that they seem to take his word on anything, even if he does not know what he is talking about? His guide detailed a past incarnation in which he

was a Senator in Rome, his name was Vibius Novius Gessius and the time was 388-328BC. He had a spirituality at that time that gave him great presence and his aura shone through to those of a spiritual ilk. When he is in a crowd now, this presence is still with him, those of any sort of spiritual persuasion will see or feel it, will recognise the spirituality shining through like a beacon and knowing of the spirituality at a level they do not even appreciate themselves, will feel able to trust and be guided by him.

Places

1. **Liking for Africa** – An enquirer felt such a strong attraction for South Africa, that he was resolved to go there to live, regardless of the trouble in the country and the fact that many that are there are trying to leave! His guide related details of a life in South Africa as a Boer farmer. His guide gave him his year of birth and death from natural causes in that life, the name of his then wife and confirmed that he had fathered three sons.

2. **Egypt** – An enquirer had a yearning to go to Egypt, not just a fancy, but a real yearning in the very depths of her being. Her guide explained that Egypt, both ancient and modern, had been the setting for many of her incarnations. Her last incarnation was there in the late 1700s and early 1800s, which had contributed to her yearning this time. In that life she was a worker on the dig when the tomb of Seti I was discovered by Giovanni Battista Belzoni.

3. **Isle of Skye** – An enquirer who usually suffers ill health went to the Isle of Skye and felt really well, something quite unusual for her. This was not just once, but had happened three times. Her guide confirmed that the scenery had triggered memories of a happy life in a place with scenery similar to that on Skye. She was also in tune with the energies of the place and this had contributed to her improved health.

4. **Liking for Spain** – A male enquirer has visited Spain and feels "at home" there, so much so that he would live there if he could. His guide gave details of a life when he was a worker with the bulls at the bull ring in Madrid in the late 1800s. Throughout that life he harboured a dream of being part of the team that fought the bull, but this was never open to him. He had thoroughly enjoyed his association with the bullring and this is what prompted his feeling of well-being.

5. **Liking Holidays on Islands** – A lady chose islands for holidays. Her guide explained that she has had several incarnations within island culture. The most recent was a life in the Hawaiian Islands as Keloni, a female incarnation in the late 1700s. She has also lived lives in what we know as the Easter Islands and the Sandwich Islands.

6. **York** – An enquirer had a particular draw to York and felt she had lived there before. Her guide confirmed that York is a destination of choice for her when she plans her incarnations. She has actually had three previous lives there. She lived there in Roman times, and was male in that incarnation. She was a carpenter by trade in that life. She lived there in the 1600s and was the daughter of a merchant and eventually the wife of another, and she lived there in the early 1900s. In that life she was the daughter of a naval seaman, whose wife remained in York with her children while he was at sea, because she felt acute homesickness if ever she left the place. It is this life that has particularly given her the feeling for the place.

7. The daughter of the enquirer above also had the same feelings about York and asked her guide for the explanation. It transpired that she was in fact the mother mentioned above, the wife of the naval seaman who could not leave the place without acute homesickness. They have shared other lives too.

Relationship Issues

1. **Difficulty with Relationships** – A male enquirer has difficulty with relationships. His guide confirmed that this is a recurring theme throughout many of his incarnations, and one which it is hoped he will improve on in this incarnation. He has a tendency to find the grass greener on the other side of the fence, which usually leads him into problems.

2. **Uneasiness in a Marriage** – An enquirer was having difficulties within her marriage and had the feeling that she had shared a life with her husband before and that the difficulties now were an echo of the difficulties then. Her guide told her that she had known her husband in a past incarnation in which they had a business connection and in which she, a male that time, had been let down badly by him. She had recognised this at some deep level. Her guide advised that after the current uneasy time all will be well if she decided to stay the course; events were actually happening exactly as planned.

3. **Unable to Commit** – An enquirer was having difficulty in her life due to her boyfriend being unable to commit to her. His previous relationships had usually ended due to his inability to commit in them too. Her guide explained that in a past life he was poorly treated by a partner to whom he had opened his very soul. This feeling of insecurity within a relationship stems from that, and he may well not be able to commit to another in this life, unless he were willingly to seek past life therapy.

4. **Compulsion to Help a Certain Person** – A male enquirer was at a loss to explain his compulsion to help a particular friend on a physical level, even though he wished he could stop doing so. His guide confirmed a past life connection with the man. The friend was his son in a previous life. In that life the enquirer was a sailor, Francisco de Aeranda. He died at sea on the 1492 voyage of Columbus, and his wife, suffering a melancholy state,

never recovered and succumbed to a fever, thus leaving the child to fend for himself. In the current incarnation, the enquirer has, at a deeper level, a wish to fulfil the duty of care he was unable to fulfil in that life.

ANIMALS

Animals do not suffer the same form of spiritual amnesia as do humans on incarnation, so it is much easier for them to recognise spiritual presence, not having first had the difficulty of shaking off our childhood conditioning. Many animals have an acute awareness of spiritual presence. This develops to a greater level in those animals, who share the lives of spiritually attuned humans. Our cat who is described in chapter six, has amazing attunement; her character is so much affected by her past life memories, she is more a cat in appearance only.

CONCLUSION

The reader may recall from previous books, my own past life influences. My occupation and hobby in this life have a resonance with occupations in past lives. Not everyone's job and interests have automatically a past life explanation, but certainly a talent which shows itself early in life can be a big clue to having done that thing at least once previously.

If one adopted a scientific stance, the cases I have listed here cannot be said to be representative of the whole population, as they were self-selected in that the enquirers have been consciously aware of something about themselves that could not be explained conventionally. The people concerned will have probably been older spirit, having sufficient acceptance or degree of enquiry (or the ability to respond to a prompt from spirit), to seek mediumship for an explanation. Being older spirit, of course, they will have had more incarnations and so more likelihood of accumulating experiences with the potential to impact on a subsequent incarnation.

There is no need to become obsessed about past lives and attributing to them the explanation for every character trait. Equally, past lives should not be dismissed as an over-imaginative explanation for our emotional selves, our likes and dislikes and our predilections.

The headings I have used show the facets of our characters where past lives can have a surprising explanation. This is an explanation that is not part of conventional thinking so far, but an area worthy of academic research once science breaks free from its "Enlightenment" straightjacket. Reincarnation is the mother of all counter-intuition. The topic, along with life-plans, merits inclusion in all human behaviour courses if we are to understand the complexity of ourselves. To repeat two of my favourite lines of poetry:

> *"Our deeds travel with us from afar*
> *And what we have been, makes us what we are."*

Spiritually, we are the sum total of all our many lifetimes, the experience and knowledge we have gained on our journey through the stages and levels. We suffer on incarnation blockage of past life memories, but full memory is, I am told, restored to us on return to spirit. In our natural state of spirit we can access at will the memory of our previous lives, just as we can earlier episodes of our present life if we so choose.

In the future a respected branch of counselling will be centred around recognising past life issues as a source or explanation for current life problems. Unfortunately there are few actual practitioners at present, and not a great deal of acceptance, but the change in both these areas has already started and will increase as more and more people realise that past lives are not the ravings of the deluded or not quite sane, but a very real aspect of our experiences and make-up and that they can explain the otherwise inexplicable aspects of our characters and personalities.

The guides tell me that the acceptance of having had past lives is an important stage for the world to reach in order that it can "graduate" spiritually. The more people bring knowledge of past lives to others once they have memory of them for themselves, the more this important change can be achieved. Reincarnation does make a nonsense of our keeping a separateness and a sense of difference between nations and regions. We have given mediumship to spirits who are currently British, but have been, for example, North

American, South American, Japanese, Russian, German and a part of many ancient cultures.

History takes on a "living" character when past life memories are accessed. The North American native Indians who were so decimated by contact with the White Man, for example, were so written out of the world script, but we have encountered many spiritual people currently British who have at least one past life as a native North American. As in theatre, the scenery and props may change but the spirit actors do not.

Past lives can occasionally be the explanation for a health problem. Illness is a complex subject and I now devote the next chapter to that aspect of destiny.

CHAPTER FIVE

PERSONAL ILLNESS

WHY GET ILL?

I have made the astonishing statement that serious illness is always planned by spirit when designing a life-plan. In many cases, serious illness is a catalyst to spiritual growth in the sufferer or those close and that will be its purpose. However, there are complexities within that explanation, some of which I would now like to explore, and to look at this topic in more detail, including how healing works and some case studies.

One writer on spiritual matters, Diane Cooper, has written that, "we cause our own diseases and to accept this". I believe that statement requires slight modification and that it would be more correct to say that spiritually **you attract to yourself the disease that you need**! Indeed, we have met a former NHS doctor, who now treats patients homoeopathically outside of the system and who uses precisely that expression. But what does it mean? Without further qualification of the statement, one could suppose illness is a punishment, or another incorrect conclusion might be drawn.

What is meant is that there is a spiritual reason for the illness, which will assist you in some way as part of your destiny. In some life-plans, a certain illness or disability can be instrumental in leading one to a pathway or discovery that one would otherwise not have found. In that case, you could be said to have attracted a disease that you need to guide you.

Another scenario can be that by understanding why or in what way you might be creating or attracting a disease, you discover something about yourself that you have hitherto not known or refused to face up to. Illness therefore can be a tool often applied in life-plans for the events they lead to, rather than just for the suffering they cause to the victim and to those around them.

When written into a life-plan, long term illness or disability provides a wealth of experiences. That expression may cause apoplexy to one who has suffered or been affected indirectly! This is again an instance of the huge change in perspective that is required in order to understand the spiritual reasoning. To explain this, one must think what the sufferer of any long-term illness or disability experiences. Depending on the severity of the illness or handicap, the following are some of the emotions and experiences that the incident can provide:

- ❖ Fear, worry, trepidation and apprehension.
- ❖ Anger, resentment, self-pity, rejection.
- ❖ The experience of not being in control of one's own life.
- ❖ Reliance on others.
- ❖ Learning the difficult task of accepting care, difficult for one who is always the one to give it.
- ❖ Courage and determination.
- ❖ Confusion and bewilderment.
- ❖ The struggle to remain informed when all around you people are talking "about you" rather than "to you".
- ❖ The battle with the system in so many scenarios.
- ❖ The need to stand up for one's self to the very people who think they are caring for one.

Those that offer care, even those dedicated to the caring professions, can all too often, become desensitised to the needs of the very people they are caring for. They are apt to make decisions and arrangements, knowing as they do, that this is best for their patient, and doing so with only the patient's welfare at heart, but they forget that the patient is a person. That person needs explanation, wants to be treated as a person with a brain capable of understanding the mysticism that surrounds the medical treatment they are receiving; may wish to know what is wrong with them, happening to them and why!

This does not just apply to modern day medical care, but has been the way for a long period. In the present day, this comes about mainly through the pressures of the time; in earlier times, it came about more because those giving medical care did not believe the patient should know what was occurring, and most patients were too intimidated to ask!

Much of the above list does not just relate to those in modern times receiving medical care, but relates to those suffering long-term illness or disability from the earliest times, and receiving care of any description from another. It is only when one is the receiver of care, rather than the giver, that these things are properly understood.

Whilst it may be of little comfort to a sufferer in the incarnation to know it, once the spirit has left the body, it is free of any illness or deformity. This would be so, of course, as that was only relevant to the shell it occupied during the incarnation. What the actual spirit required, was the lessons, the emotions, the experience of the illness or deformity and all its associated problems and traumas, and this it retains. Indeed, the gathering of this information may have been the whole reason for the incarnation, and once returned to spirit, this information and details of the life will be added to all other lives and information gathered by that spirit and all other spirits. Illness is a tool on nursery worlds, and does not feature at all in higher evolved ones. Again, this may be of little comfort.

FINGERPRINT MEMORY

We have encountered some people for mediumship whose medical problem has been diagnosed spiritually as a "fingerprint memory" brought forward from a previous incarnation. In these cases, the illness or deformity has gone, but the knowledge of it has not. Later, when reincarnation into the same life form again takes place, particularly if it is quite soon spiritually (in our terms two hundred or so years) the memory can come through with the spirit. It is only the memory, the knowledge, and in the incarnated state this manifests itself as unexplained pain or disability. The fact that the spirit "knows" it is misplaced and inappropriate to the life-plan is what so often makes the incarnated one seek understanding of it, an instinctive rebellion against it, without knowing why. An inner knowledge of the plan again, and knowing that the plan did not include this! Either that or evidence of the guide at work and all of this is most often without the person being aware that this is what is occurring.

Of course, it may have been in the plan that this happen, as a means of awakening a spiritual search, and in this case it will not

be inappropriate! One further point here, it is possible to
incarnate into another life-form in between these incarnations,
and still resurrect the remembered illness or disability when one
finds oneself in the same life-form again.

Let us bring in one or two examples of "fingerprint memory"
illness. I have mentioned this first one in the past lives cases. We
had a lady enquirer who had right shoulder tendonitis and lower
back pain that remained even after corrective spinal surgery. She
had received healing for these problems, but the pain still
remained. Her guide explained that both of these conditions, and
various other aches and pains, had a past life connection for her.

In a previous life, she had a fall resulting in paraplegia, and
the shoulder injury and injury to her lower back were the most
severe of her many injuries. In this incarnation, the surgery and
other healings have corrected any physical problem that provided
the cause in the current incarnation for the reappearing
conditions. What was now required advised the guide, was
treatment for the inherent pain from the past life injuries. This
could be achieved, he said, through spiritual contact via
meditation in which our enquirer should request that the past life
fingerprint, which was causing the residual pain even though the
condition was successfully treated, should be removed. In
meditation, her guide will succeed in removing the fingerprint of
pain, which she carries from the past.

A second illustration involves a lady whose hobby was once
body building, something she has forsaken for more spiritual
pursuits. She asked about her bad neck, back and shoulder pain
which she had suffered for some years. She had tried just about
every alternative therapy, including some unfamiliar to me.

Her guide explained that she has the physical pain from a past
life fingerprint, which she has exaggerated by her body building in
this incarnation. In 1650, the English under Cromwell defeated a
superior Scottish army under David Leslie at the Battle of
Dunbar. After being initially outmanoeuvred, Cromwell made a
surprise night attack. Retrieving the initiative, he destroyed
Leslie's army and secured access to Edinburgh. She and her third
in that life were both soldiers fighting under Leslie in that battle,
and she was badly wounded, suffering injury to her back. She
survived, but had terrible pain in her back and neck and loss of
strength in both arms from the injuries.

In subsequent incarnations, she has sought to optimise her strength, and her physical prowess, something left with her from the distant and unrecognised memory of weakness. The body building in this incarnation was the manifestation of it in this lifetime; one of her life lessons in each incarnation in which it has occurred since the weakness has been to realise in the incarnated state, that this obsession with bodily strength is unimportant, that it is strength of character and spirituality that is the important issue. Unfortunately, until this life, she has failed in this each time; her guide was delighted that in this life, she has voluntarily given up the pursuit of it in favour of a spiritual pathway; she has in fact, met the challenge and passed it in this life.

Her guide then went on to detail the cure because now she had the detail relating to the reason, it would be easier to tackle. The answer lay, as it so often does, in self-healing and visualisation. The guides realised that these were two areas she had tried, but without the information just given, she would have at best enjoyed limited success.

VISUALISATION

The same lady was given instruction on how to combat her problem using visualisation, and this makes a good blueprint for anyone to follow. What she was instructed to do, was to enter a state of relaxation and visualise herself as Corbin, a young man in his late twenties, fighting in the Battle of Dunbar for the Scottish army. It is night, and he is fighting alongside his friend, Donald. . He is struck down from a blow to his back from behind, and lies there for the rest of the battle, in which Donald is killed.

In the visualisation, she was told to isolate her current pain and confine it to the past life, acknowledging the source of it, and allowing it to go, stating that she knows it has no place in her current life. She should then visualise wrapping the afflicted areas in a blanket of orange, and as often as she can "check" that the blanket has not slipped. She should make sure the blanket is in place before leaving her bed each day, and check on it periodically throughout the day. She should repeat the visualisation and the letting go as often as she can in the early stages, daily if possible. The need for this will lessen over the months, to once a week, once a month and so on. This together with her own self-healing techniques should help her enormously her guide said. He added that she should not be concerned if she falls asleep during the exercise, as she will enter a state that is akin to meditation. She should allow herself to go where her guide takes her, and if this is sleep then this is what he judges she needs at that time. Once she has set the visualisation in motion, he will continue it as he deems necessary, even if she sleeps through the remainder of the procedure.

COMMUNICATION AND ILLNESS

On a related point, how do we reconcile the fact spirit can make a medium aware of pain in a certain part of the body that was linked to death in the incarnation, if the spirit is free of all illness? This is a frequent feature of some mediumship. The answer is that in many cases, when a medium works without great clarity, or "feels" their way with a new vibration, something like a pain or physical condition is the easiest thing for them to pick up when they first get the contact. This is particularly so in evidence mediumship, as I have called it. Spirit uses it as a way of announcing themselves.

I can relate here some personal experiences of my partner Angela. Angela's mother died of a certain brain disease that among other symptoms, caused her vocal chords to cease to work. This in turn gave rise to her experiencing a choking problem and requiring an emergency tracheotomy, with subsequent loss of speech. Following her death, Angela consulted mediums, feeling herself too emotionally involved to try for the contact personally. When they received the spirit that was her mother, they felt a problem with their throat and voice. Later, when Angela herself was visited by the spirit that was her mother, she coughed involuntarily, and felt the need to keep trying to clear her throat. Her mother used the symptom of her illness as a sort of calling card by way of identification.

Angela and I were once staying in a flat that was one of four created out of an old house, previously used as a doctor's surgery for the locality. The lounge of the flat, we later discovered, had been a consulting room. One morning, I experienced a most noticeable headache, similar to one associated with a hangover, but which puzzled me, as I had not been indulging the previous evening. I then felt a spirit vibration unfamiliar to me. I am not quickly aware when a spirit is contacting me, but the headache got my attention quite effectively! I then asked Angela to speak to the spirit. The instance served as an example of the use of a physical symptom by spirit where it is easier for the incarnated one to receive than other forms of contact.

The story of the encounter is this. The spirit's name was John Edwards and he related that he did not normally visit the house now in his spirit state, but he had been a regular attendee when it was a doctor's surgery, some forty years previously. This was because he unfortunately suffered from a brain tumour from which he eventually died, and it was the pain of his regular headache that he had allowed me to experience in order to get my attention! He seemed unsure of why he had not returned to spirit (as he should), but appeared to be well ready to do so, which we think was the reason he came to enlist our assistance. We sent him love and light form our earth energies site, using visualisation, and he was helped on his way back to spirit. The heaviness he had brought with him to the flat, his former surgery, then noticeably disappeared.

I hesitate to include this little incident in the book for fear of being considered of unsound mind, but decided that those who are spiritually aware might appreciate the event, and those unaware will be most unlikely readers, so have done so. Angela said that with the content of the book being about reincarnation and life-plans, including the fact that we plan our own illnesses and disabilities, why should I possibly think that this little incident alone would have people question my sanity!

AURAS

Let us now look at the connection between illness and the energy field or aura that surrounds us. Certain people in history have stumbled across part of the answer to illness without fully understanding the problem. In the sixteenth century Paracelsus (1493-1541) developed a theory about the link between disease and the energy of the stars. This was further developed by Dr Franz Mesmer (1734-1815), the man who gave his name to hypnotic effect. He speculated that there was a universal fluid which pervaded the Earth and all human beings, which he named "animal magnetism". He believed this invisible magnetic fluid to be affected by the planets and when its distribution became unbalanced, pain or disease resulted. The logical next point was that if the balance in the body could be restored, then cures would result. He came very close to the theoretical basis for alternative or complementary therapies centuries before their current popularity.

What he thought of as invisible magnetic fluid was the life energy that pervades all living things and the planet itself, and he was basically correct in the relation of this to disease. In modern times, there is now research evidence of the fact that pain and illness are in the energy field before it enters the body. Dr Valerie Hunt records this in her book *"Infinite Mind"*. The tests involved looking at brain waves, blood pressure changes, galvanic skin responses, heartbeat and muscle contraction simultaneously with auric changes. It was found that changes occurred in the aura before any physical systems changed.

It follows from this, that knowing that major illness is part of a life-plan, then all serious illness is encoded in the aura on birth awaiting activation, which can either be a single or a combination of life-events to trigger it, or the intervention of the guide.

That is why those that are predestined to experience a major illness or disability will do so. There are those who prove the exception to exposure to "high risk factors" in fatal illness and those who succumb with little exposure. Life-plan will have a part to play in the explanation. What is unhelpful are the regular "scare stories" in the media of an increased likelihood of fatal illness linked with particular foods, for example, without looking at other possible (spiritual) explanations.

One of the life-events that can be the activation for illness encoded in the aura at birth, is a sudden accident. In some cases the accident is the activation required to trigger a pre-planned illness. Not all accidents are in the life-plan. Some are the result of a "wrong place, wrong time" situation, where as a result of freewill choice, one finds oneself caught up in someone else's accident.

In those situations, any injury or illness resulting will appear in the aura from slightly before the time of the trauma. This corresponds to the time when the guide first realises what is going to occur and sets about his rapid rescripting. However, in the latter event, the degree of illness or injury is often (not always) far less than that suffered in an intended event. Remember also, if an accident is written into the life-plan and following the accident there is serious illness, then that too, will most likely have been written into the life-plan.

NUTRITION

Of course, whilst a major illness or disability is a planned experience, there are things we can do to help stay healthy. Many people are now looking seriously at their nutrition. Here is what we were told by spirit:

"As your race has evolved, it has developed an ever worsening diet, in short, it is gradually poisoning itself. More and more people are coming to the conclusion that they should consider their diet as key in their general health, and this is part of the change in the vibrational consciousness of the planet.

Vegetarianism is not necessary; a carnivorous diet is quite natural and acceptable. The health of some is best served by a diet that is not weighted with meat and other proteins, but this is due to their physical make-up and is biological rather than spiritually required; there are none on your planet that need to exclude meat. If they do so on moral, religious or ethical grounds, they have the freewill choice to do this, but it is not required spiritually that they do. Their ethics are a little misplaced if they become vegetarians for 'spiritual' reasons.

One of the main things for all on your planet is to eat more food prepared fresh and with natural ingredients, and eat less pre-prepared and processed foods, which are chemical laden and of little nutritional value, but there is a growing awareness of this too."

HEALING

Let us now look at healing. In simplified terms, if an illness is encoded in the aura, then it can be removed by the guide if it is spiritually correct that he should do so. I am sorry to disappoint, but need to emphasise that it must be correct in relation to the life-plan for this to occur.

I wrote in my second book, that the basis for all alternative therapies is the patient's own spirit guide at work, although many of the practitioners will be unaware that is how the treatment works. **This is in fact what healing is, all healing. All healing comes from the guide, with other helpers if he feels he needs them.** We have covered the fact that all healing, whether it is crystal, colour, Reiki, reflexology, or a whole sheaf of alternative therapies, actually comes from the guide. What is happening is that the guide, with "technical assistance" from "specialist helpers", if required, is altering the coding of the aura so that the illness may improve or be completely cured. Only the guide can do this or authorise it to be done, as only the guide knows if it is correct for a cure or improvement to take place for the life-plan.

All contact and all healing is filtered through one's own guide. However, other spirit helpers do come to lend their assistance. It may be that the guide passes this on, or he may transmit healing energy from the other spirit directly. An illustration is a healer called Leslie who asked if she had other helpers with the healing besides her guide. Her guide replied that she had received help from a Chinese gentleman, who specialised in disorders of the liver and bowel. She had received help from a North American who specialises in cancer treatment and also from a Victorian gentleman who is particularly effective in conditions such as arthritis. There have been others too.

A logical question might then be, if a person requests healing is that a sign that the time is right for it to be given? Most definitely, and quite often so, is the answer. Requesting healing is not always the key to the time being right for it to be given. One may request healing on a "I've tried everything else, so I might as well give this a try" basis. This would not show acceptance of healing, spiritual truths or anything close. The "I'll have healing and I do believe, but I will still try mainstream treatment just in case there is nothing in it" approach may not mean the time is right either.

As in all things, there are many different ways for this to be written into a life-plan. Even if one is fully accepting of healing and has no doubts at all about it, it may still not be correct for the guide to supply it, if it was not in the life-plan for healing to occur. A guide that provides healing for one who required to suffer or die from a condition, would actually be doing a disservice in spiritual terms, difficult though that may be to accept in human terms.

In many cases, however, reaching the point when one genuinely asks for healing in the full belief that it can work, or using visualisation to heal oneself again, believing in this completely, indicates to the guide that the time is right to provide it if it was planned that it should be provided. Just to complicate things further, it can also be planned that a non-believer can receive healing in order to start him on the spiritual path, so again, there is no easy way to second guess this.

In spiritual healing, where the healer is said to work "intuitively", the patient's own guide works closely with the guide of the healer. Who better knows what ails the patient than his own guide? As mentioned, some healers will work with a group of spirits for diagnosis and treatment alongside his or her own guide. This will not be a set group, but will be ever-changing, depending on the condition he is confronted with. It is most likely that the healer's own guide will be a skilled healer who would call upon the services of "specialists" in many fields. Of course, the healer himself may be unaware of what is happening at the spiritual level, he may not have clear and precise communication, but receives "thoughts" to indicate the problem with his or her patients.

Some healers are aware when healing that their guide has stepped back and someone else has come forward. This is the phenomenon of enlisting the help of a "specialist" in a particular condition. It may be one who specialises in the treatment of cancer, back troubles, blood disorders or so on. The "specialist" will be allowed through, still under the supervision of the healer's own guide, to give the special treatment, and this is when the healer feels his own guide step back or feels a change in the energy with which he is working. The guide never leaves the healer, but allows others to administer through him and so through the healer. A similar phenomenon can occur in mediumship when our guide allows another guide or a departed one to speak direct to an enquirer through Angela.

It is well known that there is a mind-body connection, that emotional issues can produce physical symptoms. There will be a consequence in that they, too, will reflect in the aura. Sometimes they can still be in the aura quite some time after a trauma was experienced, as a "fingerprint". Some healers will include an emotional cause in their diagnosis, the need for forgiveness, for example. This is what they are picking up from the patient's aura.

If a person has suffered emotionally for a long enough period, even though the issues are resolved and the person may achieve understanding and forgiveness, in the aura will remain a fingerprint that needs eradicating. It may improve of its own accord with time, provided one manages to avoid sliding again into anger or resentment, or in some cases, healing is required to remove it.

The consequences of positive and negative thoughts for our health, are beginning to be publicised. I was fascinated with Robyn Welch's book *"Conversations With the Body"*. She has the rare ability to actually see inside the human body and diagnose from its energy field, and restore both. To me, she is the medical practitioner of the future, although that will still be a long way off. Working on the energy field is the basis of application of the guide's intervention in alternative therapies. It will not be widely known for some time, that alternative therapies are really just differing means of enlisting the guide to change the aura coding.

A final point is that spirit will perform surgery on a person, sometimes without their knowledge, to prevent their early departure from the incarnation. We encountered a lady of advanced spirituality who knew she had died from a heart attack. She had experienced some stress in her life and had been overworking. Her heart just gave up. However, it was not time for her to go; she had not achieved her life-plan. Her guide, with others, operated on her aura with the result that her heart began to work again. She knew she had died as she had looked into the bathroom mirror and seen herself as a spirit. Because of her spiritual awareness, she knew she had received this help. Our guide advises that this can often happen, it is just the majority of those concerned are unaware of it.

CASE STUDIES

Let us now look at two case studies. These relate to older spirits who have consulted us for mediumship. They are not therefore generalised explanations for illness, but ones specific to the particular enquirer.

1. We have a friend who has suffered a brain tumour, not just once, but three times. The first two were removed by surgery. The doctors would not use surgery a third time. Understandably the lady is most perplexed about why she has had to repeat the experience. She asked her guide for an explanation.

    He explained that she had, to date, experienced many lives in a caring capacity. She has been the equivalent of a nurse or doctor on many, many occasions. What she has never before experienced in any great degree, however, is the other side of the coin. He went on to say that in the schedule of lessons that lead to spiritual growth, it is necessary to experience both sides of love. One must be a giver of care and a receiver of it; the giver of mother love and the receiver of it, and so on. It is also necessary, of course, to experience the situations where these things should be given or received and are not, so that one may learn by comparison.

    Her guide related that she has had little illness or disability in her lives to date. She already knew of one of her past lives from previous mediumship with us. Her name was Flora. She was with the original party of nurses that crossed the sea with Florence Nightingale to nurse the wounded in the Crimea. She had been extremely seasick, battered and bruised on the crossing. She had arrived to live in squalid conditions and to face the animosity of doctors who did not want her there. Many returned, disappointed and disillusioned, but she had stayed and assisted in the setting up of a hospital at Scutari. She was invalided home from the hospital by 18 November 1855.

    In other lives she has experienced death from sudden accident or illness, and there have been other minor health issues throughout her many lives, but she has had little experience of a long-term health problem. Having had many lives on the side of the giver, this lady planned this time to experience some of the experiences I previously listed. The reoccurrence of the illness over a period of time has given her even more opportunity, explained her guide, to experience these things.

There was a second explanation too, which is quite particular to this lady, who is an older spirit nearing the end of her journey of many lifetimes. This fact explains this second purpose. She planned in this life that she would allow her spiritual self to materialise and because of her many caring and nursing incarnations, her natural choice to do this was that of healer.

Her guide went on to say that some of the very best healers are those who suffer themselves as this gives them an insight not experienced by all, into the true nature of illness of the physical body and enables them to assist others on a higher level. (The late Mother Teresa spoke this sentiment to the late Diana, *"To heal other people you have to suffer yourself".*)

In her case, her guide further explained, it was planned that she would come to the point of searching for an alternative to the orthodox treatment for her tumour, and again this is part of the reason for her having it reoccur. If the first surgery had been successful, there would be the end of it. Surgery was still the obvious choice the second time, but it is only now, when surgery is no longer an option and radiotherapy is suggested, that the real search for an alternative is dawning on her.

It was planned that she would seek alternative healing for the tumour in the first instance, and so experience that which she in turn will be able, should she wish, to give to others. This alternative was to be in the form of earth energies used and directed by a group who had learned their powers and how to apply them. Having benefited herself from healing with the group, it is intended that she learns visualisation from the group, and will use this in self-healing and in healing of others in due course, should she decide to pursue this route.

2. A second case study involves another spirit that is much travelled. I say that to explain that the problem is not a common one and nowhere features in medical textbooks! This person is sensitive to emotion and spiritual vibration

changes, both her own and others around her. It is a little like subtle motion causing travel sickness in some. Let us further explain how this is affecting her.

When you sleep, your spiritual vibration changes subtly to allow your guide to communicate with you, although you are most often completely unaware of either the change or the communication. In this state, thoughts and ideas can be introduced; one may often have that feeling of an elusive dream that one would like to remember. It is there, just beyond the edges of memory, but try as you might, you can't recall it. You think it might have been important, but the detail escapes you. This is often the sign of a guide working during sleep.

When you first wake, in the seconds while you hover between sleep and consciousness, your spiritual vibration readjusts for the day ahead. Let me say quickly here, that the vibration does not really change, each spirit entity, both those incarnated and those in the spirit state, has its own vibration which never alters. To give an earthly example that might illustrate this complex point; think of a tape player. You insert a tape and press record, or you insert the same tape and press play; you may press fast forward or rewind or stop. The tape is the same, it has not altered, but the function it is being asked to perform does. So it is with the spiritual vibration. It does not alter, but the function it is performing does, and in those first waking moments, the function changes to what is required for the time ahead.

This is how it is for most. For a few highly evolved spirits, the vibration change may be stronger in them and the body they inhabit feels it. The body feels it, but the mind usually does not register this. This is not the case for all spirit of the same evolution, just for some. The effect of this is to cause, either digestive problems, bowel problems or headaches in the body concerned, sometimes for just an hour or so, sometimes for longer; in this enquirer's case, just the morning.

When it lasts the whole day, it is because she has received a double dose of it, by feeling the vibration shift when spiritual input is received during the day. This is not to say these are the only days she receives spiritual input, but just that these are the only days her body feels the shift. It is more usual for a body to feel the waking shift, because of its inactivity. When one is busy and otherwise occupied, it is less likely that the shift will be noticed if and when it occurs.

The timing of this problem beginning for this person coincided with the time when her guide Michael first began really working with her to develop her spiritual interests. The good news is she will grow out of this as her spiritual pathway unfolds. Some of the things she will be involved with will teach her the way to balance and centre herself so that she can control this problem. She has begun to learn this with Reiki, but there is more for her to learn yet.

Once she has learned to do this and control the problem, she will also know how to control the problem if she is affected by such a change in others. Often, as a medium, when you give a reading a similar change (not the same, but similar), occurs in the recipient. The medium needs to be able to prevent herself being affected in this way so that when she begins to work for others, she is not open to their vibrational shift.

The reason for her having this in her life-plan, is purely to facilitate her greater understanding of spirit and communication; to open her to greater information, and when she has control, to allow her to see the power the informed mind can have over the body the spirit inhabits. This is all necessary teaching for her eventual destiny, her guide advised.

QUE SERA

How can the individual tell that his illness is an intended event, that somehow this has not been contracted unintentionally? Our guide answered and said illness is almost always in one's life-plan. He did not refer here to the common cold or a case of upset stomach, but to serious, either fatal or life-changing illness.

Even in a severe outbreak of some dreadful disease, the majority affected severely will have used this as a prop to some other lesson in their life. If there were to be an outbreak of

Smallpox, one of the worst scourges our planet has known, a good quantity affected would have planned it this way. The few that suffer a serious, life-changing illness by virtue of being in the wrong place at the wrong time, are comparatively few in number. (Remember here, all is relative; even 5% of the planet's total population for all time would be a large number, while still only being 5%!)

In summary, comparatively few suffer serious or life-changing illness unless they have so planned. How do you tell in the incarnated state if it is intended? Quite simply, you do not. You may be able to see lessons learned either by the sufferer or those intimately connected, but this is more likely to be seen by an outside observer than by those actually involved. Those extremely aware of spiritual destiny may see the spiritual path or realise that they are involved by accident, but there is no formula for telling this, only by enquiry of spirit.

GLIMPSES OF THE FUTURE

The abilities not yet developed by humans are many. I will discuss these in a later book. For now, let us consider healing as being one of these. Our guide advised,

"There is a growing acceptance of it and a growing number of practitioners. Healing on your planet at present is as medicine was in its infancy, light years away from what it can become. Who would have thought, even in the 1800s when medical advances first began to be seriously made, that in this comparatively short time, medicine would have become what it is now. Healing is currently in the 'pre 1800s' stage of its development and has further to go than 'accepted' medicine ever will."

For example, there is great promise from the advances in understanding the DNA code. Certain experts are predicting disease that is in the DNA can be corrected and people need not suffer. This is true, but it will only work where it is in the life-plan for it to work. In time, there will be an increasing amount of success with this type of treatment. It is one of the ways the planet will become free of illness as Earth leaves its nursery world status.

179

To bring this about, more older spirit are incarnating here, who have it in their life-plans to bring new healing knowledge and techniques to the planet. I can give two glimpses of how healing will evolve, taken from our mediumship casebook. The first case concerns something completely new that will be directed towards the mentally challenged,. The second one concerns a spirit surgeon specialising in the treatment of MS. Here are the details.

We met a couple (thirds) who had reached the point of wishing to both leave mainstream careers and work in a spiritual way together. The husband has suffered health problems that caused him to have long periods of sick leave. It was clear to him that the illness was related to his work environment and so he was considering pursuing his case to a tribunal. He also recognised that there was a message delivered to him through his ill health, which was that it was time for him to move into a new and more spiritual area.

Upon enquiry, their guide confirmed that they both have the potential within them to be healers and workers with light. They both have many past lives incorporating healing work, either spiritually or in a more grounded manner. They have ahead of them the potential to work with an entirely new method of administering spiritual healing. The guide advised them that all healing comes from the same source. The practitioner may use Reiki, reflexology, or any other means termed alternative therapy. The method is not important; in each case, they are using the same energy, it is just the method of application that is variable. In their case, however, the method of application will be entirely new. It will be given to them when they are ready to use it. They will feel themselves guided to the way of it. It will focus around the active use of light and visualisation.

This is to be a new method of administration of healing light the guide advised. He said that it was necessary for them to arrange the material side of their life first, before they were given the new information. They are to be the ones to introduce it for the use of others. The healing light may be used for any type of disability or illness, but will have particular benefit to the mentally challenged.

It is a fact that there are many more who will incarnate with what will be viewed as mentally related disability, no matter what label society attributes to the condition. This new method of working will be of particular benefit to such persons. This new form of healing is to be their unique contribution to the spiritual knowledge of the planet.

As I carefully include in the briefing to our mediumship, the guides will not tell fortunes; our destinies are for us to find. There appears to be an exception to the rule if that is a spiritual destiny! This couple were given details of how it is to be achieved: *"Initially, and in order to achieve perfection in the application it would be correct for them to work on a one to one basis, or with small groups in a healing circle. This will be in the area of direct treatment for individual conditions,"* said their guide. *"When they are completely familiar with it, they will move into the running of workshops and the supply of literature and other materials, aimed at teaching others the use of the application. The application itself will be given to them through visualisation when they have cleared their space and are ready to begin. They may give it a name they deem appropriate as the guides had no preference in that,"* he continued, but was sure to reiterate that they did have freewill choice in this. Needless to say, they did not feel that they had any choice at all but to follow this path!

I now turn to my second glimpse of future developments. We had an enquirer who, amongst other complaints, suffered from MS. She had received spiritual healing for this and was told by her guide that she was cured, although it would take a while for all the symptoms to go completely. Having asked about a scan, her guide replied that the symptoms would be undetectable by scan, and the medical profession would most likely assume misdiagnosis in the first instance.

She went on to ask her guide if she had a special healing gift. Here is the reply: *"She has a strong healing gift. This is why she will be able to be a spirit surgeon on the earth plane in future. She will be a specialist in the area of MS, having an understanding of it from the point of view of sufferer. Surgery channelled from spirit is able to treat more than conditions that are operable on the earth plane. She will use her gift to treat 'surgically' the symptoms of MS. She will also have success with spiritual surgery for conditions of the digestion and bowel."*

A third case study involved the use of "old knowledge". What we term New Age is, in fact, very much forgotten skills from the past. We had a lady enquirer who was quite aware spiritually.

She had practised healing and meditated during which she saw images. One of these was of a being with white flowing hair and possibly a beard. Her guide confirmed this and went on to explain that this is a being often with her. He is a teacher and when on Earth was a healer and a worker with earth energies. He was a Druid and had strong spiritual connections. The lady, given her love of flowers and botanicals, could have success in the use of these for healing. She could work in what we will loosely term a "Pagan" way. This being would be the one to lead her in this work with the permission of her guide, should she ever decide to accept the role. She has freewill choice in this, but would have great success with it she was told.

CONCLUSION

It was part of the world plan that science came into the ascendancy with the Enlightenment movement of the seventeenth and eighteenth centuries. Advances in medical knowledge were an important aspect to science's progress, reinforcing its dominance in the world view mankind had of itself. All the suffering medicine alleviated showed the benefit of science and the view became widely held that all problems, especially all medical problems, could be solved with the application of enough effort and research. It was just a question of time, many thought, before we have a cure for every major disease.

But science has not proved all-solving. In addition some new problems have come along, the AIDS virus for example, and now in 2003 the SARS virus. In the West, stress has been identified as the cause of illness in itself and a contributory factor in some fatal problems such as heart disease. Stress has a paradoxical spiritual message for us. It has become recognised as a product of the mind, and as such is a learning experience for the western attitude, in that the mind is seen as the cause of dis-ease! Having learned this, then it may become recognised that the mind also can be the route to the cure of dis-ease.

A great start has been made on this new path in the increasing use of complementary therapies to reduce stress, and activities such as yoga and tai chi specifically directed at calming our minds. Visualisation has been touched upon in this chapter. Its importance has yet to be recognised as a spiritual means for bringing results for medical conditions. A big hurdle is to have a belief in its effectiveness, a belief which goes hand in hand with spiritual awareness and acceptance. Its increased practice will be part of the vibrational lift of the planet itself.

CHAPTER SIX

ANIMAL SPIRIT

A significant proportion of homes have one or more pets. Why is that? Pets do not have the sophistication we have as humans. Pets give us love; sometimes we may feel it is conditional on food and shelter, but although of lesser intelligence, they practice unconditional love more than do we, the owners. They are a great "tool" for learning about love, the giving and receiving, and expressing it openly. This is why they are often part of our life-plans. Some people can be seen to have a greater emotional bond with their pet or pets than their family relatives. Pets are, of course, also consistent in their affections. They do not imitate our behaviour patterns over divorce, for example, giving out their love to both former owners. In mediumship, we have encountered spirits who in previous lives, had only known real affection from their dog!

CAT IN BLACK

We have a black and white cat named "Sox", who is most interesting spiritually, as you might expect, given her owners! She can see spirit, which is not unusual for a pet, as many can. She has been our pet several times in previous lives and also in the current lives, again not unusual. What we have noticed in her is behaviour that is out of place for a cat.

We know from the teachings of our guide that animals may incarnate as any animal as long as they stay within category, so for instance, a mammal will always be a mammal (other than man, which is a different category for reasons we have explained earlier in the book), a reptile will always be a reptile, a bird a bird and so on, but a cat may be a cat in the current incarnation, a dog in the next and an elephant in the last.

So we wondered, was this unusual behaviour perhaps due to past life memories? As this is the first time we have spotted the possibility of past life memory in an animal, of course we had to check it out with our guide.

The list that follows, illustrates how an animal can reincarnate to the same owners and also how they experience a multitude of differing incarnations:

1. **Dog** – Sox will lick the eyelashes of Angie when she is asleep. The pet dog she had as a teenager, a Daschund named Strudel, used to do this. When Sox takes a leap and lands on the floor, she issues a growl sound. Angie's dog used to do the same. When we return from a trip out, the cat runs to the door to greet us just like a dog, and most unlike a cat! When we stayed in a flat for a while, the cat ran up and down the corridor for amusement, sending the rugs flying. She also runs around our deck on the boat having a "mad half-hour" dog style. Say her name out loud, and her tail instinctively wags. She often turns her head to look at it in amazement, as if it is acting independently of her. It is quite involuntary though, you can almost see her trying not to do it, but being compelled to nevertheless. She also chases her tail occasionally.

2. **Mongoose** – We had a tray of eggs on the kitchen worktop at a time when Sox, as far as we were aware, had never seen an egg. Sox lifted one out with a paw, let it roll and drop onto the floor, then licked at the yolk. She will also eat scrambled or hard boiled egg, but much prefers it raw. If Angie is breaking eggs into a bowl, she gets really excited and doesn't know whether to try and climb in the bowl after them or the bin after the shells!

3. **Leopard** – Sox will occasionally stretch out as if lying on the branch of a tree. She does this whilst we are eating. In playing with her, she will pretend bite as many cats do, but she also wraps her two front legs around the hand or arm, as if a big cat holding its prey.

4. **Monkey** – After canine, this is the most common past life memory in her. She likes the smell of fruit, melon, banana etc, but surprises herself by not liking the taste. You can see her getting excited when you are cutting or peeling it, and then if you offer it to her, she gets really excited, tastes it, then looks at it with her head on one side. You can almost hear her thinking, "I thought I would like that".

   She will sometimes move with her back arched, bouncing on all four legs simultaneously. She is at home jumping on my back or shoulder and riding there. She is intensely curious, investigating every new object that comes within range. She talks, or rather , she croaks or chirps. She is endlessly playing "football" with a sweet wrapper or similar object, batting it with her paw, then chasing it. Chastise her and she will "answer back".

5. **ET Life** – She has a fascination with burning candles and the smell of incense. She often sits and poses in a "china cat" position. We are told she shared a life elsewhere when Angie and I were guardians of a special spiritual site.

6. **Unknown** – She has an intense interest in dripping taps and will walk around the edge of the bath whilst one is in it. We have not identified which water liking mammal she once was, but otter has been suggested.

   She likes meditation music and piano pieces and has learned to turn off a CD she doesn't like by walking on the top of the player causing the CD to eject. We experimented with just three CDs, two calming meditation music and one rock music. She only ejected the rock music one, but always ejected it, so we know it was no accident.

In the film *"Men in Black II"*, Fred the pug remarks *"Just remember, I am only a dog in this incarnation"*! He also expresses his resentment at "canine profiling" by his primate, black-suited detective companion. As I have noted previously and others too, the Steven Spielberg films are in fact closer to the truth in places than to the fiction they appear to be. Now just how did the scriptwriter arrive at that quip about dog profiling?

ANIMAL TRAUMA

Just as can humans, we have also discovered that pets can bring past life trauma memories back with them. Sox, if she is kept shut in a room for a long period, can show signs of distress on our return, sometimes triggering a bout of obsessive-compulsive behaviour. This consists of knowingly clawing our curtains expecting a reaction (and looking over her shoulder in puzzlement if one is not forthcoming) and then seeking affection after we verbally or physically react.

We asked our guide if there was a reason for this and he advised that in a previous incarnation as a monkey, she had been caged for long periods and mistreated by her owner. Being kept confined in this life triggers the trauma memory.

We have similarly discovered trauma memory as the explanation for unusual behaviour in a friend's dog. Whenever there is a loud noise or a lot of spiritual energy in the house (which there often is), the dog will compulsively dig at the carpet in a corner or at the edge of the room as if trying to dig her way out. This behaviour has been with her since birth, and was a real puzzle to the family until mediumship revealed the reason. The dog had incarnated as a dog at the time of World War Two and experienced a life belonging to a mistress who was taken prisoner by the Japanese in the Far East. The dog had been in the prisoner-of-war camp with its mistress, who was shot along with others. At that moment there was a release of traumatised spirit and the dog frantically dug at the camp's perimeter fence trying to escape. Any loud noise reminiscent of the shooting or the presence of spirit energy are now triggers for the trauma memory in this life. The condition is helped with spiritual healing and alternative therapies, including "Rescue Remedy", from the flower essences.

We have given mediumship to enquirers who have been told of a destiny treating animals spiritually. It is little appreciated that animals can benefit just as much as humans. It would also seem another instance of our pets showing us the way. If animal spiritual healing surgeries are established, it will help their sceptical owners perhaps gain acceptance of alternative therapies as well as relieving animal suffering without drugs or surgery. After all, any improvement in animal health can hardly be written off as "the placebo effect" or "all in the mind because the recipient wants it to work".

TRUE COMPANIONS

Having obtained in March 2003, photographs of spirit orbs, I can confirm animal orbs in close proximity to human ones, proving our pets are never far away from us! I have said pets can reincarnate to the same owners. What I can further add is that the timing of their arrival and departure can be spirit influenced. Our friend had a dear spaniel whose body had worn out. The dog had a heart attack and it was intended she leave incarnation in the month (November), that it occurred. The guides decided the owner needed time to adjust to the thought of her leaving, which she did not do until early February. In April she was drawn to see a litter of puppies. One came forward and she had a feeling that this was the spirit of her previous dog. What confused her was the fact that the puppies had been born in January, which was before her beloved pet's demise, so could not possibly be a reincarnation. The guides confirmed, unlike humans, the spirit is not present at conception in the case of animals. Also, the third and spirit guide of her departed pet had "stood in" for the spirit of her old dog, until she had returned to spirit, and then she incarnated immediately. Pet and owner are now happily together again after only a two-month interval!

FINAL WORDS

Now is the time of some of the greatest challenges facing humankind. At the time of writing (March 2003), the world news media saw the credibility of the United Nations, the unity of Europe and the moral issues over war with Iraq, as the greatest challenges the world faced.

These events and scenarios are merely the beginning, the opening scene in the next act of the play called "Planet Earth". What is intended to happen is that over the coming years and decades more events with an even greater intensity of response will occur until such time as new thinking does come to the fore and prevail, and old thinking and ways of looking at the world and interacting with each other change. Change will be not just for the better, but change to bring in new horizons and new plateaus of existence and way of life for all humankind. But before that can happen, the old ways must be truly discredited and discarded. This is the learning experience for the population as a whole, not just the enlightened minority.

Although still comparatively few in number, some individuals have experienced their own changes in their current lifetime. These are ones who have a destiny working spiritually in some way. They have taken the great leap of a move into uncertainty but with an inner-knowledge of their destiny. 1995 was my own "wake-up call" year, although I would hardly have described it as such at the time. 2002 was the next one. From a small, very small beginning, it is intended what is just a tiny ripple on the surface will grow and magnify into a complete sea change as more and more people find the spiritual route and change their thinking. In doing so they will allow the planet to raise its vibration and the world will move on to the next level.

As I have said in *"Why Come Back? Book Two"*, and others have documented, more and more older spirit are now incarnating on the threshold of this planetary change to help it come about. If it does not happen at the first opportunity, second and subsequent chances are in the plan for change to occur.

This is not just the changes in our healing procedures I have discussed in chapter five, but is change to our whole way of life, of thinking and of interacting with one another; change in how we choose to live our lives and govern ourselves; change that enables us to leave behind the self-centred, egotistical, warlike, fearful and other negative behaviour patterns that are a feature of nursery planets, and to become more unified, more caring, more respectful of one another, of the planet and of all life on it.

Is this change going to be some bolt from the blue? Will it be some sudden awakening? No, it will come about with our change in thinking, the mass realisation that we are spiritual beings having a human experience, that the current lifetime is just one of many, that the game of life is experience of love and not the accumulation of possessions. In 2003, to bomb the Iraqi people in order to "liberate them", was the lesson of the 1960s Vietnam War being repeated because it was not learnt the first time. Let us hope there is a quickened learning process, so repeated disasters will not be necessary for the population to elevate its thinking, so that change will be sooner rather than later!

Thank you for reading this book. I hope you have gained new insights from it or had your own insights confirmed. Please encourage the author to write further books by recommending others to buy a copy. His books are self-published and are available direct from Quiet Waters Publishing Ltd, through the internet bookseller Amazon and by order from most booksellers.

APPENDIX ONE

EXAMPLE OF SPIRIT IN LITERATURE

SHAKESPEARE'S *"THE TEMPEST"*

I have mentioned Shakespeare's subliminal spiritual messages contained in his plays for those with awareness to spot them. I set out below some examples from one of his plays, *"The Tempest"*. Of course, there are references in many of his plays, *"Hamlet"* and *"Macbeth"* particularly.

ACTION AND LINES	SPIRITUAL REFERENCE
The meeting of Miranda, who has only known life on an island, and Ferdinand, who arrives there by a shipwreck, is an unlikely circumstance. Miranda actually says, *"This is the third man that e'er I saw,"* to alert the audience to the point.	Arranged meeting of THIRDS
It is love at first sight. The feeling is mutual. Ferdinand says, *"I'll make you the queen of Naples"*.	Love at first sight can often be the case for thirds meeting as strangers, destined to be life partners.
Prospero, Miranda's father, deliberately puts obstacles in Ferdinand's way as a test of his resolve and affections.	Obstacles are sometimes in a life-plan as a test for us.

Prospero exercises his "rough magic", for example, by his influence on the weather. *"If by your art, my dearest father, you have put the wild waters in this roar"*, says Miranda. *"I have bedim'd the noontide sun, call'd forth mutinous winds and twixt the green sea and the azured vault set roaring war,"* he admits himself.

Spirit can influence the Earth's weather. On other planets, there is group control of the weather, by incarnated spirit.

One of the invisible spirits, Ariel, speaks and it is assumed by Caliban and Stephano that it is Trinculo speaking, which he denies. *"Why, what did I? I did nothing. I'll go further off."*

The guides can speak to us through another person at times. This is the phenomenon, if you have ever experienced it, of saying something, and being surprised by it yourself.

Miranda marvels at all the people she sees for the first time, *"How beauteous mankind is! oh brave new world, that has such people in it"*.

Spirit uses the human body purely as a container. Earth is the nursery (new planet) of the universe.

Prospero calls several spirits to perform before Ferdinand and Miranda, symbolising the spiritual scripting of our lives on physical Earth, not our natural home. *"Our revels now are ended. These our actors, as I foretold you, were all spirits and are melted into air, into thin air"*.

We are spirit having a human experience. The spirit dimension is in the air around us, it is just that it is invisible to the human eye. (By the use of digital cameras, spirit orbs can now be seen).

The Great Poet gives us a description of the meditation state. The character Caliban says, *"and then in dreaming, the clouds methought would open and show riches ready to drop upon me; that when I waked, I cried to dream again"*.

We can access much through meditation – past lives; other worlds; future events.

He describes the island's unusual feature of sound. *"Be not afeard; the isle is full of noises, sounds and sweet airs, that give delight and hurt not."*

This is a description of an E.T. world, one that spirit uses where sound is a constant backdrop.

One of the shipwreck survivors, Gonzalo, speaks of their miraculous escape from drowning with the words, *"few in millions can speak like us"*.

A reference to the spiritual master himself, perhaps, with his knowledge of spirit.

Life is not what it seems, nor were some of Shakespeare's dramas intended to have one interpretation. I hope scholars will forgive my presumption.

APPENDIX TWO

EXAMPLE OF A NUMBER USED IN A LIFE-PLAN

The following details give examples of synchronicity in a life shown by the intentional use of the number nine, occasioned by the guide of John Lennon during his life.

1. Time of birth: This is recorded as being 6.30pm (6+3+0=9). Obviously the guides have limited influence and 9.00pm perhaps would have been preferred. With some small influence possible, a time that adds up to nine was second choice.

2. Date of birth: This was 9th October. Collusion was obviously needed between Lennon's guide and that of his mother. The date can sometimes be influenced by spirit if there is a planning reason to do so. The fact that Newton was born on 25th December, which had an influence on his thinking is another example.

3. Guides as we know, arrange for significant people to come into our life when we are ready. Lennon met some of the key people in his life on 9th November; Brian Epstein on that date in 1961, and Yoko Ono on that date in 1966. Another way of communicating nine, was the number of letters in the name of a person. Some other key people in his life had nine letters to their names; Mimi Smith, Jim Gretty and Bob Wooler for instance.

4. The guides will get us fixed up in our chosen careers. John's first group was called the "Quarry Men" (nine letters). Early Beatles Liverpool venues included ones with

194

nine letters; Jacaranda, Blue Angel, Cassanova. Brian Epstein secured the Beatles record contract with EMI on 9th May 1962.

5. Guides communicate all the time. A relatively early instance for John was a painting he did at the age of eleven. It showed a football player with a large nine on his shirt. Later instances included his song writing where some had a direct reference to nine; "Revolution 9", "#9Dream", and "One After 909". Others had nine letters; "Penny Lane" and "Sgt. Pepper". Some had nine key words; "All we are saying is give peace a chance".

6. Guides will pick out residences for us; not always, only if there is a spiritual significance. For example, someone who immediately feels at home on viewing a property possibly picks up the presence of earth energies, which may have relevance to why they should be there. In John's case, in New York he bought an apartment on West 72nd Street (7+2=9) and their main Dakota apartment number was also at first, seventy two.

7. Accidents, as I have said, are predestined very often. The guides collude with each other to get those who are destined to be affected together at the critical moment. John was predestined to suffer the loss of someone close to him. The car that knocked down and killed his mother had the registration number LKF 630 (6+3=9). It was driven by Police Constable 126 (1+2+6=9).

As Ralf Waldo Emmerson remarked, *"The dice of God are always loaded"!*

Information source: *"Lennon"* Ray Coleman, Pan Books 2000, pp703-705.

ABOUT THE AUTHOR

As for all of us, there is the human profile and also the spiritual one. Much of his current life was discussed *in "Why Come Back?"* the events in his life to date and comparison made with his life-plan. In the second book, *"Why Come Back? Book Two"*, the author described and gave the spiritual reasoning behind his fourteen past lives on Earth.

He is an older spirit, nearing the end of the journey of very many lifetimes, spent on the many worlds that are used by spirit. It is one of the tasks sometimes chosen by older spirit to advance knowledge in some way and this is the main plot of his current incarnation. All spirit will become teachers, it is not the privileged task of just a few; it just depends where one is on the spiritual journey.

In human terms, the author has taken a leap into the unknown with his spiritual work and largely given up the material life. Having had a professional career as an accountant, he has sold his practice, his home and many of his possessions and now lives with his partner aboard a converted wooden Scottish fishing boat, where he devotes himself to writing and to teaching small groups about spirit, life-plans, past lives, and sharing his knowledge. To this end, he has co-founded with his partner, "The British School of Spiritual Knowledge". The website can be viewed at www.bssk.co.uk.

Having completed his first book near Glasgow and his second in Northumberland, the author is currently in Hull, the intention being to move around the coast of the UK and in so doing, reach others who wish to expand their understanding and share their knowledge and ideas about why we are here.

OTHER BOOKS BY THE SAME AUTHOR

"Why Come Back?" ISBN 0-9542047-0-0

We each have a life-plan; the book describes what they are, how they are formulated, what goes into them, how they are the yardstick for review on return to spirit. The book describes what "spiritual growth" is, the object of the life-plans, which ultimately is to experience the multi-faceted nature of "unconditional love".

The book's unique contribution to greater spiritual knowledge is the introduction of the concept of the Spiritual Three, awareness of which is fundamental to learning about spirit and the spiritual journey.

Price £10.99

"Why Come Back? Book Two" ISBN 0-9542047-1-9

This gives illustrations and examples of the many incarnations of the soul including the spiritual perspective behind painful human experiences, and the spiritual explanation for the lives themselves, using the author's own past lives, supplemented by mediumship enquiries.

More detail is revealed about spirit guides, Spirit Council, spirit and time, how the future is known, what fairies are, animal spirits and much more. '

The rare quality of the author's communication is movingly demonstrated with examples of "spirit letters" of personal messages from spirit to loved ones on the earth plane.

Price £12.99

These may be ordered direct from the publisher and will be sent post and packing free to mainland UK addresses.

Please write to:

Quiet Waters Publishing Ltd
North Lodge
The Pines
Boston Road
Sleaford
Lincs NG34 7DN

THE BRITISH SCHOOL OF SPIRITUAL KNOWLEDGE

This book, together with the author's other work, forms part of the course material of the school. The school's half and one day courses include:

> **WHAT IS THE NEW AGE?** – We are bound by our human experiences and limited perceptions, largely unaware of the spiritual dimension that is around us. The New Age is in essence, a revival of ancient wisdom. This course explains what that is.

> **YOU'VE BEEN HERE BEFORE!** – Our most popular course; the chance to have your own personal evidence of the spiritual journey through a **past life regression experience**, combined with relaxation, teaching and discussion and the explanation of the regression images or teaching points, through mediumship.

> **NOTHING HAPPENS BY ACCIDENT!** – Each one of us has a life-plan and a spirit guide whose task it is to direct and prompt us into our destiny. This is a course that examines in-depth, the planning that accompanies all human life.

> **THE MEANING OF LIFE** – A change in our perspective gives us the spiritual explanation of why we are here. A course to explain the spiritual journey we all undertake.

> **MEETING ONE'S GUIDE** – Your guide communicates with you all the time. This is a course designed to encourage a two-way process so answers can be obtained to personal questions.

- ➤ **ONE-TO-ONE PSYCHIC COUNSELLING SESSIONS –** One to one sessions are offered by the hour, as a chance to put questions to your guide through mediumship. No guarantees are offered; what you can be told is the decision of the guide's alone and beyond our control. A typed transcript of the session is provided.

Please contact the school for a brochure and course availability, or view this online at www.bssk.co.uk.

The school also promotes one and two day Mind, Body and Spirit events in the East of England. For details and a schedule of dates, please e-mail events@bssk.co.uk or write to:

> The British School of Spiritual Knowledge
> North Lodge
> The Pines
> Boston Road
> Sleaford
> Lincs NG34 7DN

If anyone wishes to help in any way with the school's activities and objectives, please contact us. We welcome particularly course leaders with their own area of skill or knowledge to augment our courses and workshops.